The publication of *A Field Guide to the Wildflowers of Mexico's Copper Canyon Region* was made possible through the generous sponsorship of Robert Hirsh and Kate Ferguson, Patricia Longhurst, Phil Ferguson, Mitchell Kleinman and Margaret Ferguson, Susan Stilwell—S & S Tours, Bernie and Lynn Kinlan, Felicia Nagamatsu, Mary Sloan, Bert Malerba, Cristina Hallah—Cristina's Canyon Tours, Steve Ford and Carolyn Donahue, and JoElla Casse. In addition, many thanks to all those who made donations, attended the fundraising event, and/or preordered the book.

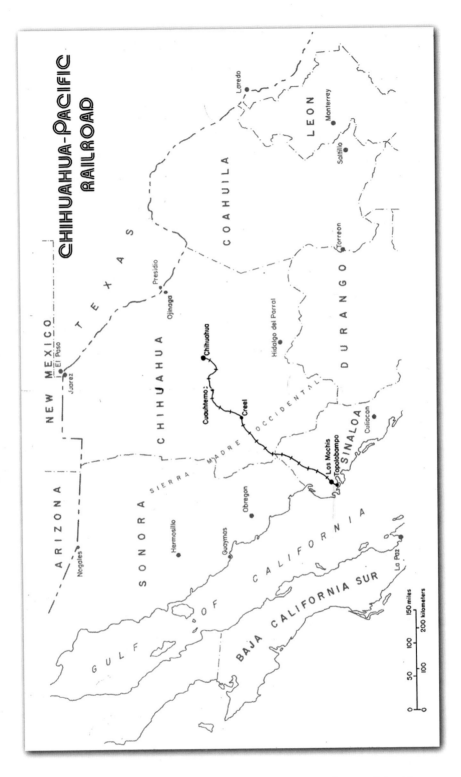

Chihuahua–Pacific Railroad Map reprinted by permission of Dr. Robert H. Schmidt, International Map Co., 1004 Cerro Azul, El Paso, Texas.

A FIELD GUIDE TO THE WILDFLOWERS OF MEXICO'S COPPER CANYON REGION

By Linda J. Ford

Contributions by Ryan J. Hawkins and Daniel Atha
Spanish translation by Toutcha Lebgue

All photographs by author and Ryan J. Hawkins unless otherwise credited. The daisy-like
flower, elongated cluster, and rounded cluster illustrations on page 14 and 16 are by Jean
Mackay. The remaining illustrations on pages 14 through 17 are used with permission
from Loughmiller, Campbell, and Lynn Loughmiller. *Texas Wildflowers: A Field Guide.*
Austin: University of Texas Press. 1984.

The Donning Company Publishers
184 Business Park Drive, Suite 206
Virginia Beach, VA 23462

Steve Mull, General Manager
Barbara Buchanan, Office Manager
Anne Cordray, Editor
Jolene Blevins, Graphic Designer
Derek Eley, Imaging Artist
Susan Adams, Project Research Coordinator
Tonya Hannink, Marketing Specialist
Pamela Engelhard, Marketing Advisor

Mary Taylor, Project Director

Library of Congress Cataloging-in-Publication Data

Ford, Linda J.
  A field guide to the wildflowers of Mexico's Copper Canyon region / by
Linda J. Ford ; contributions by Ryan J. Hawkins and Daniel Atha ; Spanish
translation by Toutcha Lebgue.
      p. cm.
  Includes bibliographical references and index.
  ISBN 978-1-57864-556-5
  1. Wild flowers--Mexico--Copper Canyon Region--Identification. 2. Wild
flowers--Mexico--Copper Canyon Region--Pictorial works.. I. Hawkins, Ryan
J. II. Atha, Daniel E. III. Title.
  QK211.F67 2009
  582.130972'16--dc22
                              2009022940

Printed in the United States of America at Walsworth Publishing Company

TABLE OF CONTENTS

Foreword

The urge to document the plants of the earth is probably as old as spoken language. A procession of brave, adventurous plant explorers, traveling at great peril and cost to the far corners of the world, has marched through history for hundreds of years. When we consider how long professional botanists from major research institutions have been searching for, collecting, and cataloging plants, surely we can conclude that by the dawn of the twenty first century, they've discovered just about all there is to find.

The project that produced *A Field Guide to the Wildflowers of Mexico's Copper Canyon Region*, however, proves that an amateur can still contribute greatly to the knowledge of the world's flora. Linda Ford, a home gardener and volunteer Master Gardener for Cornell Cooperative Extension in Rensselaer County, New York, has created the first-ever wildflower guide to a remote part of Mexico, the Copper Canyon region. While visiting the area on vacation, she fell in love with the people, landscape, and flowers, and thought that a colorful, easy-to-use field guide would be educational for visitors as well as the local people.

It's fair to say that Linda initially underestimated the task. She had to learn the language, so she enrolled in several semesters of Spanish courses at local colleges. While already a good film photographer, she had to experiment with and then master the newer digital technology. After she discovered that virtually no field guides for the area existed, Linda contacted botanists in the U.S. and Mexico, busy professionals who helped her learn how to study and describe wild plants in the field, as well as the process of attaching proper scientific names and other technical data to them. Getting this book printed and into our hands then required figuring out the labyrinthine publishing world. It all goes to show that if you dream big while traveling, you'll come home with more work than you tried to escape in the first place.

People won't value what they don't see or understand, so this pioneering book gives both a face and a voice to the wildflowers. The casual observer will start by enjoying them for their beauty, be drawn to study them more closely to learn the secrets of their composition, and finally will want to share their knowledge with younger generations. This book might even encourage those in power to work toward conserving the ecosystem of this beautiful part of the world. Not bad for an amateur who can now call herself a botanist.

David Chinery, Extension Educator

Preface

The idea of creating this field guide came out of a conversation that I had with Diego Rhodes at his hotel, the Paraiso del Oso, in Cerocahui, Mexico. After being at his ranch for a few days as a tourist and noticing fields of wildflowers, I asked him if he had a field guide of the local wildflowers. He said that none existed. I declared that I better make one. He then offered for me to come back as a volunteer/researcher and stay at his hotel. I took him up on his offer, which I will forever be grateful for, and spent the next three wildflower seasons volunteering at the ranch and researching the wildflowers of the Copper Canyon region. I was quick to discover that very little scientific study had been done in this area, which meant that identifying the flowers was going to be challenging.

Therefore, in order to create this guide and insure its accuracy, I relied on the support and contributions made by several people. My husband, Phil, has provided his undying support with this project from its inception to completion, and my family and friends have been there for me in numerous ways. Dr. Richard Spellenberg from the New Mexico State University provided me with excellent encouragement, coaching, and guidance in taking on this project. Ryan J. Hawkins, who was a Rotary International volunteer in Mexico, assisted me as a field technician, found trails to explore, and navigated the rural roadways in Mexico. Also, he has provided moral support and assistance in many other ways including setting up my website. Daniel Atha from the herbarium at the New York Botanical Garden spent many long hours diligently working on providing me with the identifications of the plants. Other botanists who assisted with the identifications were M. H. Nee, O. Kosovsky, and R. W. Spellenberg. Dr. Toutcha Lebgue from the Universidad Autonoma de Chihuahua generously translated all of the text into Spanish. David Chinery from Cornell Cooperative Extension provided resources, materials, and suggestions, but most of all he believed in me and that I could do this project. And I want to thank Manuel Gil from Batopilas, Juan Loya Rascon (Robano) from Creel, and Rúben Lopez from Cerocahui for their contributions to my research. Also, I want to thank Bonnie Dirk, a volunteer from Canada, who hiked the trails in the springtime looking for wildflowers, and I especially want to acknowledge and thank Mary Taylor Miller, Anne Cordray, Jolene Blevins, and Pamela Englehard from my publishing company who all were exceptional to work with in bringing this book to fruition.

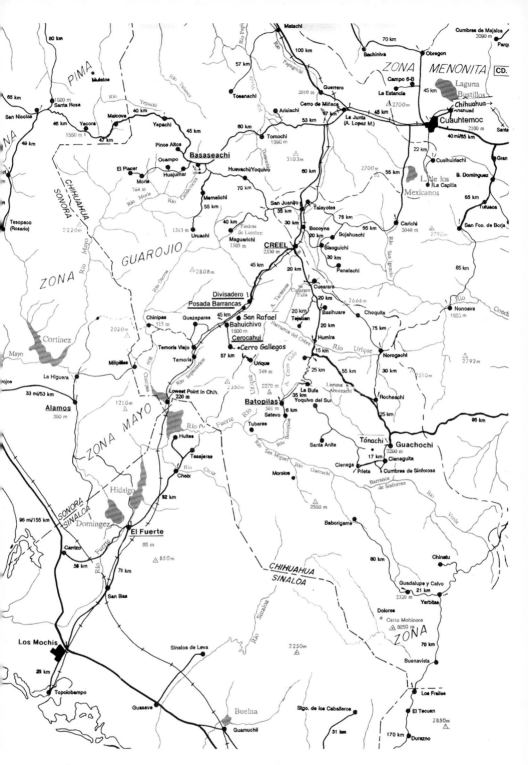

Sierra Tarahumara. Map reprinted by permission of Dr. Robert H. Schmidt, International Map Co., 1004 Cerro Azul, El Paso, Texas. The author added three locations to the map: San Rafael, Cerro Gallegos, and Tónachi.

9

About the Copper Canyon Region

Copper Canyon, located in the Sierra Madre Mountains of northwestern Mexico in the state of Chihuahua, has a very unique ecosystem and very little scientific study has been done on the flora of this area. A more proper name might be "Sierra Tarahumara" since the Copper Canyon (*Barranca del Cobre*) is but one of four massive gorges in the area covering 25,000 square miles (64,000 square kilometers).

The Sierra Tarahumara were created by volcanic activity. The deposits caused by numerous volcanic eruptions created mountains over 8,000 feet in elevation. Fractures occurred that resulted in more than twenty canyons carved out of the Sierra Tarahumara by at least six different rivers. Each of the four major gorges—*Barranca del Cobre, Barranca del Urique, Barranca del Sinforosa, and Barranca del Batopilas*—are over 5,500 feet deep.

Because of the difference in elevation from over 8,000 feet at the high plateau and canyon rims to the bottom of the canyons at 1,800 feet, four very distinct climate zones with a wide variety of vegetation have resulted.

In the highlands is the Madrean Conifer Forest with fir, pines, Douglas fir, and red Madroño trees. Going down in elevation, there is the Pine-Oak Woodland with pine, live oak, and agave. Continuing down, next comes the Arid-Tropical Deciduous Thorn Forest with scrub oak, mesquite, and cardon. The last zone located at the bottom of the canyons is the Tropical-Subtropical Riparian Forest that has fig, sycamore, ceibas, grasses, reeds, and palms.

During the winter months, the temperature can drop below freezing at the rim of the canyon while down in the canyon, the climate is subtropical. During the summer months, afternoon rains often occur. As a result of these rains, the streams and waterfalls begin to flow and the vegetation including wildflowers come to life in late August, September, and early October. This wildflower guide focuses mainly on the flowers that bloom during this peak two-month period. (It is very dry from February to June, and it is possible to see only an occasional wildflower.) In addition to abundant wildflowers in the fall, the temperatures are also more moderate at the rim as well as in the canyon that time of year.

The name, Sierra Tarahumara, comes from the Native Americans that make up 90 percent of the native culture in this region. The estimated number of Tarahumara living in the region ranges from 35,000 to 70,000.

The Tarahumara live throughout the mountains in small, scattered settlements, adapting to life in a rugged environment while preserving their native culture. They are migratory people that move to the mountains in the summer and then to the canyons where it is warm in the winter. Upon visiting the region, one can see the weaving skills of the women who make intricate baskets from long pine needles and/or sotol. The Tarahumara are also knowledgeable in the use of plants for medicinal purposes and are known for their long distance running.

The Tarahumara or their ancestors were the original inhabitants in the area. Later the Spaniards came in search of silver and gold and in search of souls to convert to Christianity. Racial intermixing occurred and the mestizo or mix-blooded people became more numerous than the Tarahumara. After the independence of Mexico in 1821, settlement in the state of Chihuahua was encouraged. It was at this point when more Mexicans moved into the Sierra Tarahumara. While mining, tourism, and forestry provide many jobs in the area, there are also many who work in clinics, schools, and stores, and others who own small businesses.

The best way to visit the Sierra Tarahumara is by the Chihuahua–Pacific Railway (Ferrocarril Chihuahua al Pacífico) that travels back and forth between Los Mochis near the Sea of Cortez and Chihuahua in the interior of northern Mexico. Access to the mountains and canyons is best done from the train stops at Bahuichivo, Posado Barrancas, Divisadero, and Creel. Good quality accommodations can be found in the Sierra Tarahumara as well as reputable guides.

How to Get There and How to Plan Your Trip

If you are traveling on your own, here are some suggestions on how to explore the Copper Canyon region.

The Copper Canyon Railroad (Chihuahua–Pacific Railway) leaves from departure points of either Los Mochis and El Fuerte on the west coast or Chihuahua, Cuauhtémoc, and Creel to the east. Refer to the map on page 9 to locate the various places mentioned. It is possible to fly into either Los Mochis or Chihuahua, take the train the entire route one-way, and then fly out of the other city. Los Mochis is served by flights from Tucson or Los Angeles whereas Chihuahua is served from Tucson, Phoenix, El Paso, Dallas, or Houston (this is subject to change). The most spectacular portion of the train ride is from Los Mochis or El Fuerte. Starting at sea level in Los Mochis, the route climbs over eight thousand feet (2500 meters) to its highest point, which is Los Ojitos located between Divisadero and Creel.

There are first- and second-class trains that run every day. The first-class train, normally used by tourists and tour groups, makes fewer stops, is air conditioned, and has a dining car. The second-class train has a slightly longer travel time, food is provided by vendors at the stations, and this train frequently runs late and could result in passing the most spectacular scenery in the dark. However, it costs approximately one-half the first-class fare.

There is a time schedule for departure and arrival but consider it a guideline because delays frequently occur. It is possible to purchase tickets at the train station or on the train the day that you travel, but this is not recommended during the busy times of the year (the Christmas and Easter holidays).

If you choose to travel independently, you have the flexibility of riding the train to the stop of your choosing, staying for a few days in one area which gives you time to explore, and then catching the next train when you are ready to continue. The four major train stops giving the best access to the canyons are Creel, Divisadero, Posada Barrancas, and Bahuichivo. From this last stop, it is recommended that you continue on to Cerocahui—a peaceful and picturesque area with hiking and horseback riding opportunities as well as guided tours to the rim and into the canyon. Each of these places provide suitable accommodations and offer tours to explore the region.

If you want to fly in and out of the same city, then you can take the train part way along the route and then back track. If you start at Los

Mochis, you should consider going at least as far as Creel, and if you start at Chihuahua, it is recommended that you go at least as far as El Fuerte in order to have the full experience of riding the train through the Sierra Tarahumara.

Another option is to take a bus from El Paso to Chihuahua and on to Creel, which may be more convenient because the schedule is more flexible than the train and less expensive than flying. The two bus lines out of Chihuahua offer large, comfortable, and air-conditioned buses. If you start at Los Mochis, you have the option of taking the local bus to El Fuerte and picking up the train there.

The third option is to drive, but it is only recommended for adventurous drivers. If you start, for example, in Chihuahua, the road is only paved as far as San Rafael. This option should only be considered if you have a sturdy, high clearance vehicle such as a pickup or SUV because once you leave the paved road, the road is very rough—filled with pot holes, large rock outcroppings, and there are stream beds to cross which could be impassable after a rainstorm.

If you prefer to travel with a tour group, there are several reputable companies. Two that I can personally recommend are Cristina's Canyon Tours (www.cristinascanyontours.com) and S & S Tours (www.ss-tours.com).

Your trip to the Copper Canyon region will be filled with spectacular scenery, comfortable accommodations, restaurants with safe food and drinking water, knowledgeable local guides, and spectacular wildflowers in the fall. Many of the flowers that you will see are indigenous to this region.

How to Use this Guide

This is the first ever field guide of wildflowers for the Copper Canyon region of Mexico. I chose the most conspicuous flowers that primarily bloom in the fall after the rainy season.

The guide is organized so that a photograph and a description of each flower are opposite each other. This format allows easy comparison of the two and facilitates identification. I have used photographs because they are the most realistic representation of the flowers growing in their natural habitat.

You will notice that the arrangement of the flowers is by color—white, yellow, orange, red, pink, purple, and blue. The two groups that were the most difficult to distinguish between were the pinks and the purples. In my final determination, I included orchid, magenta, fuchsia, mulberry, and lavender with the pinks, and in the purples are the violet flowers.

Within the color groups, I have arranged the flowers according to the physical structure of the flower and the arrangement of the flower on the stem. Within each subgroup, flowers are arranged by blossom width going from the smallest to the largest.

The first subgroup is radially symmetrical flowers. These flowers can be divided into equal halves along several lines. Some examples of radial symmetrical flowers are morning glory, dahlia, and four o'clock.

The second subgroup is called daisy- and dandelion-like flowers. These flowers have many strap-like petals. Some examples of this subgroup are zinnia, aster, and coneflower.

The third category is bilaterally symmetrical flowers. These flowers can be divided into equal halves along one line only and each half forms a mirror image of the other half. Examples of these flowers are spiderwort, day flower, and the pea flowers.

Elongated cluster is the fourth subgroup. These flowers are arranged along a stem in either a loose or dense cluster. The individual flowers in these clusters can be either radially or bilaterally symmetrical, for example, lupine, penstemon, and larkspur.

The final subgroup is the rounded cluster. The flowers are in a loose or dense rounded mass at the top of the stem. Examples of this subgroup are verbena, horsemint, and pearly everlasting.

After noticing the color, the physical structure of the flower, and the arrangement on the stem, the next thing to note are the leaves. Even though this guide is not organized according to leaf arrangement, leaf shape, and so forth, this information is included in the description as it can be an important factor in identifying the flower. For example, the arrangement of the simple leaves can be as follows:

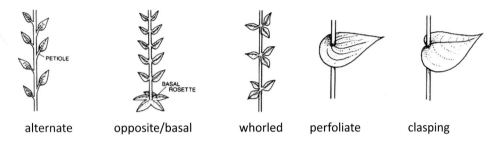

| alternate | opposite/basal | whorled | perfoliate | clasping |

The majority of the simple leaf shapes sighted in this guide are as follows:

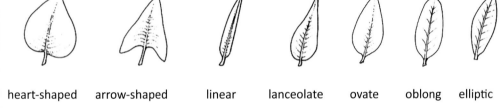

| heart-shaped | arrow-shaped | linear | lanceolate | ovate | oblong | elliptic |

Some leaf types are compound and those would include:

| pinnate | palmate | trifoliate |

And the final characteristic to notice regarding the leaves is the margins (the edges of the leaf). They can be as follows:

entire (smooth)   toothed   lobed

In most cases, I have provided the family, genus, and species. I have also included the common name when available and in some cases the Spanish name. Because very little scientific study has been done in this region, even the experts were not able to identify a few of the flowers. However, I still have included them. I feel certain that this guide will allow you to easily identify many of the beautiful and unique flowers that you will see and certainly enhance your visit to this region.

Cómo Utilizar esta Guía

Esta es la primera guía de campo de flores silvestres de la región de las Barrancas del Cobre, Chihuahua, Mexico. Elegí las más notables flores que florecen en el otoño después de la temporada de lluvias.

La guía está organizada de manera que una fotografía y una descripción de cada flor se encuentran frente a frente. Este formato permite una fácil comparación de las dos, y facilita la identificación. He utilizado las fotografías porque son la representación más realista de las flores que crecen en su hábitat natural.

Usted notará que el arreglo de las flores está en base a colores: blanco, amarillo, naranja, rojo, rosado, púrpura (morado) y azul. Los dos grupos más difíciles de distinguir fueron las flores rosas y las violetas. En mi determinación final, incluí los colores orquídea, magenta, rosa, moreras, el color lavanda con las flores rosas, y dentro de las moradas están incluidas las flores violetas.

Dentro de los grupos de colores, he organizado las flores de acuerdo a la estructura física de la flor y el arreglo de la flor en el tallo. Dentro de cada subgrupo, las flores son arregladas según su anchura partiendo desde la más pequeña hasta la más grande.

El primer subgrupo son las flores radialmente simétricas. Estas flores se pueden dividir en mitades iguales a lo largo de varias líneas. Algunos ejemplos de flores con simetría radial son: flor de la jicama, del toloache, entre otras.

El segundo subgrupo son las flores de tipo margarita diente de león o girasol. Estas flores son agrupadas sobre una estructura llamada cabezuela la cual tiene en su periferia una o varias líneas de flores representadas por un solo pétalo, reconocidas como flores liguladas. Algunos ejemplos de este subgrupo se encuentran en la familia del girasol.

La tercera categoría son flores que tienen una simetría bilateral. Estas flores se pueden dividir en mitades iguales a lo largo de una sola línea y cada medio es una imagen de la otra mitad. Ejemplos de estas flores pueden encontrar en algunas especies de las familias Scrophulariaceae, Lamiaceae, Commelinaceae, entre otras.

El cuarto subgrupo representa las flores que son agrupadas a lo largo de racimos alargados. Estas flores se disponen a lo largo de un tallo o bien en grupos sueltos o densos. Cada uno de estos grupos tienen flores que pueden ser radialmente o bilateralmente simétricas, por ejemplo, lupino, Penstemon, y Delphinium.

El último subgrupo es el grupo de flores agrupadas sobre los ápices de los tallos florales o sea arregladas en la parte superior del tallo. Ejemplos de este subgrupo son verbena y otros.

Después de notar el color, la estructura física de la flor, y su arreglo sobre el tallo, el siguiente paso es de observar las hojas. Aunque esta guía no está organizada de acuerdo al arreglo de la hoja, su forma, tamaño, etc., esta información está incluida en la descripción, ya que puede ser una característica importante en la identificación de la flor. Por ejemplo, la disposición de las hojas simples pueden ser las siguientes:

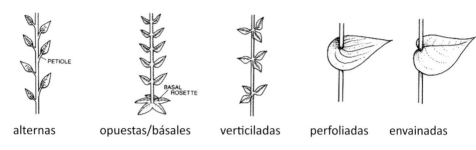

alternas   opuestas/básales   verticiladas   perfoliadas   envainadas

La mayoria de las formas de hojas ilustradas en está guía son las siguientes:

en forma de corazón   en forma de flecha   lineal   lanceolada   ovada   oblonga   elíptica

Algunos tipos de hojas son compuestas y incluyen:

pinnada   palmeada   trifoliada

Y la ultima caracteristica de la hoja para tomar en cuenta es el borde o el margen de la lamina, el cual puede ser:

entero   dentado   lobulado

En la mayoría de los casos, incluí la familia, género y especie. También he incluido el nombre común, cuando se disponga y, en algunos casos, el nombre español. Debido a que se carece de estudio científico en esta región, hasta los más expertos no fueron capaces de identificar algunas de las flores. Aun así las tengo incluidas. Estoy segura de que esta guía le permitirá identificar fácilmente muchas de las hermosas y singulares flores ustedes puedan encontrar, desde luego, mejorar y disfrutar más de su visita en esta región.

Part One White Flowers

White Radially Symmetrical

Mexican Thistle
Eryngium lemmonii
- Carrot family Apiaceae

Plant: 18" tall.
Flower: 1" wide.
Description: Radially symmetrical thistle-like plant with 9 prickly white/silver bracts surrounding tiny, violet flowers in ball-like crown in the center. Leaves alternate, 3/4–2" long, narrowly lanceolate at base, margins deeply toothed as move up the stem.
Habitat: Pasture, loam, moist, sun. Elevation 5354'.
Range: Arizona, New Mexico, Mexico.
Comments: Photographed in August near Cerocahui after crossing the Arroyo del Cerocahui in the field on the left before beginning the climb into the mountains.

- Familia de la Zanahoria Apiaceae

Planta: de 45 cm de alto.
Flor: de 2.5 cm de ancho.
Descripción: Cardo con 9 brácteas espinosas, blanco-plateadas rodeando diminutas flores violetas arregladas en una cabezuela radialmente simetrica. Hojas alternas, 1.9–5 cm de largo, estrechamente lanceoladas en la base, los márgenes profundamente dentados a medida que se sube el tallo.
Hábitat: Pastizales, suelos francos, húmedos, asoleado. Elevación 1632 m.
Distribución: Arizona, Nuevo México, México.
Comentarios: Fotografiada en agosto cerca de Cerocahui, después del cruce del Arroyo Cerocahui en el campo sobre la acera izquierda antes de la subida de la sierra.

Geranium wislizeni
- Geranium family Geraniaceae

Plant: 16" tall.
Flower: 1" wide.
Description: White and red stripes, radially symmetrical flower, 5 petals. Stamens and pistil in tight cluster then all spread out. Stem hairy, prostrate to ground. Leaves opposite, pinnately compound, 1/2–1 1/4" long. Margins lobed. Loved by bees.
Habitat: Riverbed, soil rocky, moist, sun. Elevation 7308'.
Range: Texas, southern Arizona, and northern Mexico.
Comments: Photographed in September at Choquita, 4.97 miles from Creel.

- Familia del Geranio Geraniaceae

Planta: de 41 cm de alto.
Flor: de 2.5 cm de ancho.
Descripción: Flor radialmente simétrica, 5 pétalos rallados de líneas blancas y rojas. Estambres y pistilo todos juntos al principio, pero se abren al madurarse. Tallo velludo, casi rastrero. Hojas opuestas, palmeadamente compuestas, de 1.3–3.1 cm de largo, márgenes lobulados. Preferido por las abejas.
Hábitat: Lecho de los rios, suelo pedregoso, húmedo, asoleado. Elevación 2227 m.
Distribución: Texas, sur de Arizona, norte de México.
Comentarios: Fotografiada en septiembre en Choquita, 8 km de Creel.

Mexican Thistle/*Eryngium lemmonii*

Geranium wislizeni

White Radially Symmetrical

Mexican Star, Estrella
Milla biflora

• Onion family Alliaceae
Plant: 13" tall.
Flower: 1 1/4" wide.
Description: Bright white radially symmetrical star-shaped flower, 6 petals with green stripes running the length of the underside of each petal. Each stem bears 1 or 2 flowers and a single narrow linear 7" basal leaf, margins entire. Fragrant.
Habitat: Outcroppings of rocks under trees, sand, dry, semi-shade. Elevation 5400'.
Range: Arizona, New Mexico, Texas, Mexico, Guatemala.
Comments: Photographed in August near Paraiso del Oso above Arroyo del Ranchito, near Cerocahui.

• Familia Alliaceae
Planta: de 20 cm de alto.
Flor: de 3.1 cm de ancho.
Descripción: Flores radialmente estrelladas, de color blanco claro, 6 pétalos con rayas verdes a lo largo del envés. Cada tallo con 1 o 2 flores sostenidas por una hoja, angosta linear, de 17.5 cm, márgenes enteros. Aromática.
Hábitat: Lugares rocosos abajo de los árboles, arenosos, secos. Elevación 1646 m.
Distribución: Arizona, Nuevo México, Texas, México, Guatemala.
Comentarios: Fotografiada en agosto cerca de Paraiso del Oso, arriba del Ranchito, cerca de Cerocahui.

Not Yet Identified

• Morning glory family Convolvulaceae
Plant: 7 1/2" tall.
Flower: 2 1/2" long, 1 1/4" wide.
Description: White united funnel shaped flower, radially symmetrical. Multistemmed. Opposite leaves in clusters, very narrow linear 1/4–3/4" long. Bulb.
Habitat: Open field, soil hard packed sandy loam, dry, sun. Elevation 7641'.
Range: Chihuahua, Mexico.
Comments: Photographed in September after turning left into San Ignacio, 4.5 miles from Creel.

• Familia de la jicama Convolvulaceae
Planta: de 18.8 cm de alto.
Flor: de 6.3 cm largo, por 3.1 cm de ancho.
Descripción: Flor radialmente simétrica, corola unidad formando un embudo de color blanco. Tallos numerosos. Hojas opuestas, agrupadas, estrechamente lineares, de 6 mm–1.9 cm de largo. Bulbo presente.
Hábitat: Campo abierto, suelo compacto, franco arenoso, seco, asoleado. Elevación 2329 m.
Distribución: Chihuahua, México.
Comentarios: Fotografiada en septiembre después de dar vuelta a la izquierda hacia San Ignacio, 7.7 km de Creel.

Mexican Star, Estrella/*Milla biflora*

Not Yet Identified

White Radially Symmetrical

Desert Thorn Apple, Toloache
Datura discolor

• Nightshade family Solanaceae
Plant: 15" tall.
Flower: 3 1/2" long, 2 1/2" wide.
Description: Off-white radially symmetrical flower, funnel shaped, flared with 5 points, dark maroon-streaked throat, calyx 4" long. Leaves opposite and alternate, palmately lobed, 2–5" long. Margins lobed. Insects had made small holes in leaves. Plant poisonous.
Habitat: Along riverbed, rock and sand, damp during the rainy season, sun. Elevation 2080'.
Range: Arizona, California, Mexico.
Comments: Photographed in September in Arroyo Los Tachos, Batopilas.

• Familia de la papa Solanaceae
Planta: de 37.5 cm de alto.
Flor: de 8.8 cm de largo, por 6.3 cm de ancho.
Descripción: Flor radialmente simétrica, en forma de embudo, blanca, exhibiendo 5 segmentos agudos, garganta de la corola morado oscuro; cáliz de 10 cm de largo. Hojas opuestas y alternas, palmeadamente lobuladas, de 5–12.5 cm de largo. Márgenes lobulados. Los insectos hicieron pequeños agujeros en las hojas. Planta venenosa.
Hábitat: Orillas de ríos, suelo arenoso, húmedo, asoleado. Elevación 634 m.
Distribución: Arizona, California, México.
Comentarios: Fotografiada en septiembre en el Arroyo Los Tachos, Batopilas.

Spider Lily
Hymenocallis

• Amaryllis family Amaryllidaceae
Plant: 18–36" tall.
Description: White, fragrant, radially symmetrical flowers produced in loose cluster. Flowers are spider-like. Narrow, reflexed, and arching petals surround a daffodil-like cup. Basal leaves are long, strap-shaped, arching, and dark green. Bulb.
Habitat: Up from stream bed, rock and sand, moist, sun. Elevation 5471'.
Range: Chihuahua, Mexico.
Comments: Photographed in July at Tascate between Paraiso del Oso and Cerocahui. This flower has not been verified for accuracy of identification.

• Familia Amaryllidaceae
Planta: 45–91 cm de alto.
Descripción: Flores aromatizantes, radialmente simétrica, blancas, producidas en grupos. Las flores tienen forma de arañas. Pétalos angostos, colgantes y erguidos sobre un receptáculo en forma de copa. Las hojas básales son largas, erguidas, ralladas de negro y verde. Bulbo presente.
Hábitat: Orillas de río, suelo rocoso, arenoso, húmedo, asoleado. Elevación 1668 m.
Distribución: Chihuahua, México.
Comentarios: Fotografiada en julio en Tascate entre Paraiso del Oso y Cerocahui. La identificación correcta de esta flor no ha sido verificada.

Desert Thorn Apple/*Datura discolor*

Spider Lily/*Hymenocallis*

White Radially Symmetrical

Hairy Beggarticks, Bidente Piloso or Mazote
Bidens pilosa

• Aster family Asteraceae
Plant: 8–10 1/2" tall.
Flower: 3/4" wide.
Description: White radial symmetrical flower, 7 ray flowers, yellow disk 3/8" wide. Opposite, compound, toothed leaves 1 1/2" long. Medicinal plant. Fruits are aggravating to hitchhikers because they gather on their clothing.
Habitat: Bank near stream bed, rock and sand, moist, semi-shade. Elevation 5482'.
Range: Originating from South America and common in all tropical and subtropical areas in the world.
Comments: Photographed in September at the beginning of the trail to Cave of Crosses before reservoir near Paraiso del Oso, Cerocahui.

• Familia del girasol Asteraceae
Planta: de 20–27 cm de alto.
Flor: de 1.9 cm de ancho.
Descripción: Flor radialmente simétrica, blanca, con 7 flores liguladas, flores tubulares amarillas, de 9 mm de ancho. Hojas opuestas, compuestas, dentadas, de 3.8 cm de largo. Planta medicinal. Los frutos producen muchas molestias por pegarse y acumularse sobre las ropas.
Hábitat: Orillas de río, suelo rocoso, arenoso, húmedo, semí sombreado. Elevación 1671 m.
Distribución: Originalmente de Sur América y común en todas las areas tropicales y subtropicales del mundo.
Comentarios: Fotografiada en septiembre al principio de la vereda a la Cueva de las Cruces antes del tanque de agua cerca de Paraiso del Oso, Cerocahui.

White Daisy- and Dandelion-like

Erigeron fraternus

• Aster family Asteraceae
Plant: 18–24" tall.
Flower: 3/4–1" wide.
Description: White daisy-like, narrow ray flowers radiating from flat yellow 1/4" disk, 30 petals. Multi-stemmed. Elliptic, opposite, slightly toothed leaves 1/2–1" long. Margins slightly toothed.
Habitat: River valley along trail, wooded, rocky sand, moist, shade. Elevation 5630'.
Range: Durango and Chihuahua in Mexico.
Comments: Photographed in September on the trail to Huicochi (waterfall) near Cerocahui.

• Familia del girasol Asteraceae
Planta: de 45–60 cm de alto.
Flor: de 1.9–2.5 cm de ancho.
Descripción: Cabezuela formada por muchas flores liguladas de color blanco (30 de ellas) bordeando flores tubulares de 6 mm de largo. Muchos tallos desarrollados. Hojas opuestas, elípticas, ligeramente dentadas, de 1.3–2.5 cm de largo. Márgenes ligeramente dentados.
Hábitat: Orillas de ríos, a lo largo del camino, boscoso, suelo rocoso, arenoso, húmedo, sombreado. Elevación 1716 m.
Distribución: Durango y Chihuahua en México.
Comentarios: Fotografiada en septiembre sobre camino a Huicochi (cascada) cerca de Cerocahui.

Hairy Beggarticks, Bidente Piloso or Mazote/*Bidens pilosa*

rigeron fraternus

White Bilaterally Symmetrical

Mariposa
Calochortus venustus

- Calochortus family Calochortaceae
Plant: 10" tall.
Flower: 3/4" wide.
Description: White bilaterally symmetrical flower, 3 larger petals intersected with 3 smaller petals, yellow center. Basal leaves, linear, 4–6" long, margins entire.
Habitat: Moist, sun. Elevation 5625'.
Range: California, Mexico.
Comments: Photographed in August off the road on the east side between Cerocahui and Bahuichivo.

- Familia Calochortaceae
Planta: de 25.4 cm de alto.
Flor: de 1.9 cm de ancho.
Descripción: Flor bilateralmente simétrica, los 3 pétalos más grandes hacen intersección con los 3 más pequeños, centro Amarillo. Hojas básales, lineares, 10–15 cm de largo, márgenes enteros.
Hábitat: húmedo, asoleado. Elevación 1715 m.
Distribución: California, México.
Comentarios: Fotografiada en agosto sobre orillas del camino entre Cerocahui y Bahuichivo.

White Elongated Clusters

San Luis Mountain Ipomopsis
Ipomopsis pinnata

- Phlox family Polemoniaceae
Plant: 18–22" tall.
Flower: 1/4" long, 1/4" wide.
Description: White elongated cluster with small radially symmetrical flowers, 5 petals. Leaves alternate, thin needles 1/4–1" long.
Habitat: Meadow on hillside, rock and sand, moist, sun. Elevation 5424'.
Range: New Mexico and Chihuahua, Mexico.
Comments: Photographed in September on a meadow high above Arroyo del Ranchito near Paraiso del Oso, Cerocahui.

- Familia Polemoniaceae
Planta: de 45–56 cm de alto.
Flor: de 6 mm de largo, por 6 mm de ancho.
Descripción: Flores radialmente simétricas, agrupadas sobre pedúnculos largos, blancas, con 5 pétalos. Hojas alternas, aciculares, de 6 mm–2.5 cm de largo.
Hábitat: Llanos sobre lomas, suelo rocoso y arenoso, húmedo, asoleado. Elevación 1653 m.
Distribución: Nuevo México, México.
Comentarios: Fotografiada en septiembre en un llano arriba del Arroyo del Ranchito, cerca de Paraiso del Oso, Cerocachui.

Mariposa/*Calochortus venustus*

San Luis Mountain Ipomopsis/*Ipomopsis pinnata*

White Elongated Clusters

Arizona Bluecurls
Trichostema arizonicum

- Mint family Lamiaceae
Plant: 14–20" tall.
Flower: 1/2" long, 3/8–1/2" wide.
Description: White/violet elongated cluster, bilaterally symmetrical flower, 5 petals—2 on each side violet to white, lower lip wider and darker violet with white stripe, many long stamens that arch over rest of flower. Leaves fragrant, opposite, ovate, 1/2–3/4" long. Margins entire with hairs. Multi-branching.
Habitat: Along road, cut in ditch, rock and sand, arid, sun. Elevation 4200'.
Range: Arizona, New Mexico, Texas, north and central Mexico.
Comments: Photographed in September on the road to San Ignacio, 5 miles from Batopilas, Rebenton.

White Rounded Clusters

Confituria
Lantana hispida

- Verbena family Verbenaceae
Plant: 24" tall.
Flower: 1/2" long, 1/4" wide.
Description: Sprawling low-shrub, flower white rounded cluster, radially symmetrical, 5 lobed petals. Leaves opposite, ovate, 3/4–1 1/2" long. Margins toothed. White edible fruit 3/16" wide. Traditionally used in Mexico to treat tuberculosis, cough, cold, and asthma.
Habitat: Along road, rocky cliff, sand and rock, arid, sun. Elevation 4500'.
Range: Guatemala, Honduras, Belize, Mexico.
Comments: Photographed in September on the road to San Ignacio, 5 miles from Batopilas, Rebenton.

- Familia de la menta Lamiaceae
Planta: de 35.5–50 cm de alto.
Flor: de 1.3 cm de largo, por 0.9–1.3 cm de ancho.
Descripción: Flores bilateralmente simétricas agrupadas, de color blanco violáceo, con 5 pétalos: los dos de cada lado de color violáceo a blanco, el quinto inferior más grande, violáceo oscuro con rallas blancas con muchos estambres salientes. Hojas aromáticas, opuestas, ovadas, de 1.3–1.9 cm de largo. Márgenes enteros con vellosidades. Tallos con muchas ramificaciones.
Hábitat: A lo largo de caminos, en zanjas, suelo rocoso y arenoso, seco, asoleado. Elevación 1280 m.
Distribución: Arizona, Nuevo México, Texas, norte y centro de México.
Comentarios: Fotografiada en septiembre sobre el camino a San Ignacio, 8 km de Batopilas, Reventón.

- Familia del oreganillo Verbenaceae
Planta: de 60 cm de alto.
Flor: de 13 cm de largo, por 6 mm de ancho.
Descripción: Arbusto bajito con flores radialmente simétricas, blancas, agrupadas, con 5 pétalos lobulados. Hojas opuestas, ovadas, de 1.9–3.8 cm de largo. Márgenes dentados. Fruto comestible, blanco, de 5 mm de ancho. Usado tradicionalmente en Mexico para curar la tuberculosa, tos, gripe y asma.
Hábitat: A lo largo de caminos, acantilados, suelo arenoso y rocoso, seco, asoleado. Elevación 1372 m.
Distribución: Guatemala, Honduras, Belice, México.
Comentarios: Fotografiada en septiembre sobre el camino a San Ignacio, 8 km de Batopilas, Reventón.

Arizona Bluecurls/*Trichostema arizonicum*

Confituria/*Lantana hispida*

White Rounded Clusters

Huachuca Mountain Stonecrop
Sedum stelliforme

- Stonecrop family Crassulaceae
Plant: 1 1/2–2" tall.
Flower: 3/8" wide.
Description: White succulent plant, rounded clusters, radially symmetrical flowers, brown anthers that look like dots. Fleshy, red stems. Alternate leaves 1/4" long.
Habitat: Between crevices on volcanic rock, scant soil, dry, sun. Elevation 5639'.
Range: Arizona, New Mexico, Mexico.
Comments: Photographed in September near El Ranchito up on a mountain behind Paraiso del Oso, Cerocahui.

- Familia Crassulaceae
Planta: de 3.8 a 5 cm de alto.
Flor: de 9 mm de ancho.
Descripción: Planta suculenta con flores aglomeradas, radialmente simétricas, blancas, con anteras cafés parecidos a puntos negros. Tallos carnosos. Hojas alternas de 6 mm de largo.
Hábitat: En grietas sobre rocas volcánicas, suelo seco, asoleado. Elevación 1719 m.
Distribución: Arizona, Nuevo México, México.
Comentarios: Fotografiada en septiembre cerca de El Ranchito en la sierra atrás de Paraiso del Oso, Cerocahui.

Plummer's Candyleaf
Stevia plummerae

- Aster family Asteraceae
Plant: 18" tall.
Flower: 3/8" wide.
Description: White rounded cluster, radially symmetrical flowers, 5 petals. Stem of cluster originates where leaves join main stem. Opposite, lanceolate, toothed leaves 2–3 1/2" long. Margins toothed.
Habitat: Up from stream bed, rocky sand, moist, sun. Elevation 5454'.
Range: Arizona, New Mexico and Chihuahua, Durango, Sonora in Mexico.
Comments: Photographed in September on a trail to Cave of Crosses near Paraiso del Oso, Cerocahui.

- Famillia del girasol Asteraceae
Planta: de 45 cm de alto.
Flor: de 9 mm de ancho.
Descripción: Cabezuela radialmente florecida, 5 flores liguladas blancas. Tallo ramificado. Hojas opuestas, lanceoladas, dentadas, de 5–8.8 cm de largo. Margenes dentados.
Hábitat: Sobre orillas del arroyo, suelo rocoso, arenoso, húmedo, asoleado. Elevación 1662 m.
Distribución: Arizona, Nuevo México y Chihuahua, Durango, Sonora en México.
Comentarios: Fotografiada en septiembre sobre camino a la Cueva de las Cruces cerca de Paraiso del Oso, Cerocachui.

Huachuca Mountain Stonecrop/*Sedum stelliforme*

Plummer's Candyleaf/*Stevia plummerae*

White Rounded Clusters

Crusea longiflora

• Madder family Rubiaceae
Plant: 5" tall.
Flower: 1/2" long, 1/2" wide.
Description: White round cluster radially symmetrical flowers, long and narrow tube with 4 petals often curved backwards, stigma extending above each flower. Opposite, ovate leaves 1/4–3/4" long, margins entire.
Habitat: Hillside above stream, rocky sand, moist, semi-shade. Elevation 5436'.
Range: Costa Rica, Guatemala, Honduras, Mexico, Nicaragua, Panama.
Comments: Photographed in September on hillside above Arroyo del Ranchito near Paraiso del Oso, Cerocahui.

• Familia Rubiaceae
Planta: de 12.5 cm de alto.
Flor: de 1.3 cm de largo, por 1.3 cm de ancho.
Descripción: Flores radialmente simétricas, con la corola formando largo tubo con 4 pétalos a menudo doblados hacia a trás, estigma saliente de cada flor. Hojas opuestas, ovadas, de 6 mm–1.9 cm de largo. Márgenes enteros.
Hábitat: Lomeríos, suelo rocoso, arenoso, húmedo, semí-sombreado. Elevación 1657 m.
Distribución: Costa Rica, Guatemala, Honduras, México, Nicaragua, Panamá.
Comentarios: Fotografiada en septiembre sobre loma arriba del Arroyo del Ranchito cerca de Paraiso del Oso, Cerocahui.

Pearly Everlasting, Pringle's Cudweed

Gnaphalium pringlei

• Aster family Asteraceae
Plant: 8–36" tall.
Flower: 1/2" long.
Description: Plant with wooly rigid stem topped by a roundish cluster of pearly white flower heads 1/2–3/4" wide, small yellow crown. Leaves alternate, 1–1 1/2" long, narrowly lanceolate, underside hairy, margins entire.
Habitat: Edge of pasture, loam, moist, sun. Elevation 5354'.
Range: New Mexico, Arizona, Texas, northern Mexico.
Comments: Photographed in August in a field near Cerocahui, at the beginning of the road to Cerro Gallegos.

• Familia del girasol Asteraceae
Planta: de 20–91 cm de alto.
Flor: de 1.3 cm de ancho.
Descripción: Planta con un tallo rígido, leñoso, terminado por flores aglomeradas en cabezuelas de color blanco perla, de 1.3–1.9 cm de ancho, pequeña corona amarilla. Hojas alternas, de 2.5–3.8 cm de largo, angostamente lanceoladas, peludas en el envés, márgenes enteros.
Hábitat: Pastizales, suelos francos, húmedos, asoleados. Elevación 1632 m.
Distribución: Nuevo México, Arizona, Texas, norte de México.
Comentarios: Fotografiada en agosto en las afueras de Cerocahui, al inicio del camino a Cerro Gallegos.

Crusea longiflora

Pearly Everlasting, Pringle's Cudweed/
Gnaphalium pringlei

White Rounded Clusters

Lemon Mint, Horsemint
Monarda citriodora

• Mint family Lamiaceae
Plant: 13–18" tall.
Flower: 1" long.
Description: Rounded cluster with 3 or 4 whorls of flower heads, deep lavender bracts grow at base of whorl and 6 white to lavender 2-lipped bilaterally symmetrical flowers on top of each whorl. Leaves opposite, 1–2" long, linear, margins entire. Entire plant and flowers smell minty.
Habitat: Near stream, rock outcroppings, sand, moist, sun. Elevation 5409'.
Range: Southern U.S., northern Mexico.
Comments: Photographed in August across the road from Paraiso del Oso near the Arroyo del Cerocahui.

• Familia de la menta Lamiaceae
Planta: de 33–45 cm de alto.
Flor: de 2.5 cm de ancho.
Descripción: Planta con 3 o 4 verticilos de cabezuelas, brácteas de color lavanda oscuro y 6 flores bilabiadas de color blanco a lavanda, saliendo de cada verticilo. Hojas opuestas, de 2.5–5 cm de largo, lineares, márgenes enteros. Toda la planta expide un olor a menta.
Hábitat: Cerca de arroyos, suelos rocosos, arenosos, húmedos, asoleados. Elevación 1649 m.
Distribución: Sur de US, norte de México.
Comentarios: Fotografiada en agosto sobre camino a Paraiso del Oso, cerca del Arroyo del Cerocahui.

Lemon Mint, Horsemint/*Monarda citriodora*

Part Two Yellow Flowers

Yellow Radially Symmetrical

Mexicana Yellow Star-grass
Hypoxis mexicana

• Lily family Liliaceae
Plant: 7" tall.
Flower: 1/2" wide.
Description: Yellow radially symmetrical 6 petaled flower, 6 prominent stamen. Narrow basal linear leaves 2–7" long. Bulb.
Habitat: Bank near stream bed, rocky sand, moist, sun. Elevation 5482'.
Range: Arizona, Mexico, Argentina.
Comments: Photographed in September at the beginning of the trail to Cave of Crosses before the reservoir near Paraiso del Oso, Cerocahui.

• Familia Liliaceae
Planta: de 17.5 cm de alto.
Flor: de 1.3 cm de ancho.
Descripción: Flor amarilla, radialmente simétrica con 6 pétalos (tépalos), 6 estambres salientes. Hojas lineares, básales, de 5–17.5 cm de largo. Bulbosa.
Hábitat: Orillas de arroyo, suelo rocoso, arenoso, húmedo, asoleado. Elevación 1671 m.
Distribución: Arizona, México, Argentina.
Comentarios: Fotografiada en septiembre at principio del camino a la Cueva de Las Cruces antes del deposito de agua cerca de Paraiso del Oso, Cerocahui.

Buffalo Bur, Duraznillo
Solanum rostratum

• Nightshade family Solanaceae
Plant: 16–31" tall.
Flower: 3/4–1" wide.
Description: Yellow star-like radially symmetrical flower, 5 petals united with projecting stamen beak. Leaves 2–6" long, blades deeply parted into irregular pinnate lobes. Stem covered with golden yellow spines. This plant is highly toxic.
Habitat: Small open area above stream, moist, sand, sun. Elevation 5330'.
Range: Southwest/Plains U.S., Texas, Mexico.
Comments: Photographed in August along the bank of Arroyo del Cerocahui near Paraiso del Oso, Cerocahui.

• Familia de la papa Solanaceae
Planta: de 41–79 cm de alto.
Flor: de 1.9–2.5 cm de ancho.
Descripción: Flor amarilla, estrellada, radialmente simétrica, 5 pétalos unidos, con estambres salidos. Hojas de 5–15 cm de largo, laminas profundamente partidas en segmentos irregulares. Tallos cubiertos de espinas doradas. Esta planta es altamente toxica.
Hábitat: Área abierta arriba del arroyo, húmedo, arenoso, asoleado. Elevación 1625 m.
Distribución: Llanuras del Suroeste de USA, Texas, México.
Comentarios: Fotografiada en agosto a lo largo del Arroyo del Cerocahui cerca de Paraiso del Oso, Cerocahui.

Mexicana Yellow Star-grass/*Hypoxis mexicana*

Buffalo Bur, Duraznillo/*Solanum rostratum*

Yellow Radially Symmetrical

Cuban Jute, Arrowleaf Sida
Sida rhombifolia

- Mallow family Malvaceae

Plant: 14–16" tall.

Flower: 3/4–1" wide.

Description: Multi -stemmed plant, pale yellow radially symmetrical flower, 5 petals. Opposite, lanceolate, toothed leaves 1–2 1/2" long. Margins toothed. Medicinal plant.

Habitat: Next to riverbed, rocks and sand, moist, shade. Elevation 5610'.

Range: Grows in over 70 countries throughout tropical, subtropical, and warm temperate zones.

Comments: Photographed in September at Tascate–El Cajón trail, Cerocahui.

- Familia del algodón Malvaceae

Planta: de 35–41 cm de alto.

Flor: de 1.9–2.5 cm de ancho.

Descripción: Planta con tallos numerosos, flor amarilla pálida, radialmente simétrica, 5 pétalos. Hojas opuestas, lanceoladas, dentadas, de 2.5–6.3 cm de largo. Márgenes dentados. Planta medicinal.

Hábitat: A las orillas del arroyo, entre rocas, suelo arenoso, húmedo, sombreado. Elevación 1710 m.

Distribución: Se encuentra en casi 70 países en los trópicos, subtrópicos, y zonas templadas calidas.

Comentarios: Fotografiada en septiembre sobre el vereda a Táscate–El Cajón, Cerocahui.

Helianthemum chihuahuense

- Rockrose family Cistaceae

Plant: 10–12" tall.

Flower: 3/4–1" wide.

Description: Yellow radially symmetrical flower, 5 heart shaped petals, 1/4" stamens that lay flat against the flower. Woody stem. Alternate, narrow lanceolate leaves 1/2" long, margins entire.

Habitat: Along rocky trail, dry, sun. Elevation 5690'.

Range: Chihuahua, Mexico.

Description: Photographed in September on descending from vista at Tortuga, near Paraiso del Oso, Cerocahui.

- Familia Cistaceae

Planta: de 24–30 cm de alto.

Flor: de 1.9–2.5 cm de ancho.

Descripción: Flor amarilla, radialmente simétrica con 5 pétalos en forma de corazón, estambres de 6 mm de largo acostados sobre los pétalos. Tallo leñoso. Hojas alternas, angostas, de 1.3 cm de largo con márgenes enteros.

Hábitat: A lo largo de la vereda rocosa, seca, asoleado. Elevación 1734 m.

Distribución: Chihuahua, México.

Comentarios: Fotografiada en septiembre bajando de Vista a Tortuga, cerca de Paraiso del Oso, Cerocahui.

Cuban Jute, Arrowleaf Sida/*Sida rhombifolia*

Helianthemum chihuahuense

Yellow Radially Symmetrical

Sisyrynchium pringlei
- Iris family Iridaceae

Plant: 14" tall.

Flower: 1" wide.

Description: Yellow star-like radially symmetrical flower, 6 petals, flat stem. Two flat leaves coming out from base, 5–7" long, linear, margins entire.

Habitat: Open area on top of slope, sand and red clay, moist, sun. Elevation 5651'.

Range: Chihuahua, Michoacan, Sinaloa, Durango, and Jalisco in Mexico.

Comments: Photographed in August off the east side of the road between Paraiso del Oso and Bahuichivo, near Cerocahui.

- Familia Iridaceae

Planta: de 35.5 cm de alto.

Flor: de 2.5 cm de ancho.

Descripción: Flor estrellada, amarilla, radialmente simétrica, con 6 pétalos, tallo aplanado. Dos hojas planas saliendo de la base, de 12.5–17.5 cm de largo, lineares, márgenes enteros.

Hábitat: Lugares abiertos sobre faldas, arenosos y arcillosos, húmedos, asoleados. Elevación 1722 m.

Distribución: Chihuahua, Michoacan, Sinaloa, Durango y Jalisco en México.

Comentarios: Fotografiada en agosto sobre orillas del camino entre Paraiso del Oso y Bahuichivo, Cerocahui.

Arizona Beggarticks
Bidens aurea
- Aster family Asteraceae

Plant: 30–40" tall.

Flower: 1 1/2" wide.

Description: Two-toned, yellow radially symmetrical flower, lighter on outside, darker inside, 5 petals, 1/2" disk with brown tips. Multi-stemmed. Opposite, divided palmately compound leaves 1–2" long. Margins can be toothed or entire.

Habitat: On stream bank, sand, moist, sun. Elevation 5528'.

Range: Arizona, north and central Mexico.

Comments: Photographed in September on the trail to Cave of Crosses near Paraiso del Oso, Cerocahui.

- Familia del girasol Asteraceae

Planta: de 76 a 102 cm de alto.

Flor: de 3.8 cm de ancho.

Descripción: Cabezuela con flores, radialmente arregladas, amarillas pálidas en las afueras y mas oscuras por dentro, con 5 flores liguladas, flores tubulares de 1.3 cm de largo con puntas cafés. Tallos numerosos. Hojas opuestas, palmeadamente segmentadas, de 2.5–5 cm de largo. Márgenes enteros o dentados.

Hábitat: Orillas de arroyos, sobre suelos arenosos, humedos, asoleados. Elevación 1685 m.

Distribución: Arizona, norte y centro de México.

Comentarios: Fotografiada en septiembre sobre camino a la Cueva de las Cruces, cerca de Paraiso del Oso, Cerocahui.

Sisyrynchium pringlei

rizona Beggarticks/*Bidens aurea*

41

Yellow Radially Symmetrical

Yellow Evening Primrose
Oenothera flava

• Evening primrose family Onagraceae
Plant: 8" tall.
Flower: 1 1/4" long, 2" wide.
Description: Pale yellow single radially symmetrical flower, 4 petals with green stripes, calyx folding together to form a scoop, prominent stamens, green pistil. Basal, linear leaves 8–9" long. Margins deeply toothed.
Habitat: Open field, soil hard packed sandy loam, dry, sun. Elevation 7641'.
Range: Western U.S., Mexico.
Comments: Photographed in September after the left hand turn into San Ignacio, 4.5 miles from Creel.

• Familia Onagraceae
Planta: de 20 cm de alto.
Flor: de 3.1 cm de largo, por 5 cm de ancho.
Descripción: Flor solitaria, radialmente simétrica, amarilla, 4 pétalos con rallas verdes, cáliz en forma de una copita, estambres prominentes, pistilo verde. Hojas básales, lineares, de 20–22.5 cm de largo. Márgenes profundamente dentados.
Hábitat: Campos abiertos, suelo compacto, franco-arenoso, seca, asoleado. Elevación 2329 m.
Distribución: Suroeste de U.S., México.
Comentarios: Fotografiada en septiembre después de la vuelta a la izquierda a San Ignacio, 7.7 km de Creel.

Arizona Rosemallow
Hibiscus biseptus

• Mallow family Malvaceae
Plant: 8–10" tall.
Flower: 2" wide.
Description: Pale yellow radially symmetrical flower, 5 petals, throat blackish maroon, center orange disk 1/2" tall, 5 white stamens, many pointed calyx. Lies close to ground, hairy stem. Leaves alternate, heart shaped, some lobed, 1–1 1/4" long. Margins toothed.
Habitat: Shoulder of road, halfway down canyon, rocky, arid, sun. Elevation 3979'.
Range: Arizona, New Mexico, Mexico.
Comments: Photographed in September on the road to Batopilas, at km marker 21 from paved road.

• Familia de Algodón Malvaceae
Planta: de 20 a 25 cm de alto.
Flor: de 5 cm de ancho.
Descripción: Flor radialmente simétrica, amarillenta, 5 pétalos, con la garganta morado, con el centro anaranjado, de 1.3 cm de largo 5 estambres, cáliz con muchos sépalos puntiagudos. Planta casi rastrera, tallo peludo. Hojas alternas, en forma de corazón, algunas lobuladas, de 2.5–3.1 cm de largo. Márgenes dentados.
Hábitat: Orillas de camino del cañón, suelo rocoso, seco, asoleado. Elevación 1213 m.
Distribución: Arizona, Nuevo México, México.
Comentarios: Fotografiada en septiembre sobre camino a Batopilas, km 21 del camino pavimentado.

Yellow Evening Primrose/*Oenothera flava*

Arizona Rosemallow/*Hibiscus biseptus*

43

Yellow Daisy- and Dandelion-like

Wright's Snakeweed
Gutierrezia wrightii

- Aster family Asteraceae

Plant: 18–23" tall.
Flower: 1/2" wide.
Description: Yellow daisy-like flower, 1/8" wide disk, 19 petals. Multiple stems. Alternate, narrow linear leaves 1–2 1/4" long, margins entire.
Habitat: Up from stream bed, sand and rocks, moist, sun. Elevation: 5471'.
Range: Arizona, New Mexico, and Chihuahua, Sinaloa, Sonora, Mexico.
Comments: Photographed in September at Tascate up from a stream bed, near Paraiso del Oso, Cerocahui.

- Familia del girasol Asteraceae

Planta: de 45 a 58 cm de alto.
Flor: de 1.3 cm de ancho.
Descripción: Cabezuela con flores radialmente arregladas de color amarillo, flores tubulares de 3 mm de ancho, 19 flores liguladas (pétalos). Tallos numerosos. Hojas alternas, lineares estrechas, de 2.5–5.7 cm de largo, márgenes enteros.
Hábitat: Orillas del arroyo, suelos arenosos, rocosos, húmedos, asoleados. Elevación 1637 m.
Distribución: Arizona, Nuevo México, y Chihuahua, Sinaloa, Sonora, México.
Comentarios: Fotografiada en septiembre en Tascate, orillas de un arroyo, cerca de Paraiso del Oso, Cerocahui.

Polymnia maculata

- Aster family Asteraceae

Plant: 16–20" tall.
Flower: 5/8" wide.
Description: Yellow daisy-like flower with 7–10 petals surrounded by 4–5 green bracts. Leaves arrow-shaped, 1" long, opposite, toothed. Leaves form a bridge with dark red veins in the center, flower stems radiate from center of bridge at main stem. Rough hairs on rigid stem. Margins toothed.
Habitat: Side of river stream, moist, sand, semi-shade. Elevation 5432'.
Range: Guatemala, Panama, Belize, north and central Mexico.
Comments: Photographed in September along the bank of Arroyo de El Cajón, Cerocahui.

- Familia del girasol Asteraceae

Planta: de 41 a 50 cm de alto.
Cabezuela: de 1.6 cm de ancho.
Descripción: Flor en cabezuela formada con 7 a 10 pétalos dispuestos en forma radiada, de color amarillo con 4 a 5 brácteas verdes. Hojas en forma de flecha, de 2.5 cm de largo, opuestas, dentadas, provistas de nervios de color rojo oscuro, márgenes dentado; los tallos florales dispuestos en forma radiada en el centro del tallo principal, coriáceos al tacto.
Hábitat: Orillas de arroyo, suelos húmedos, arenosos, semí-sombreados. Elevación 1656 m.
Distribución: Guatemala, Panamá, Belice, Norte y centro de México.
Comentarios: Fotografiada en septiembre a lo largo del Arroyo el Cajón, Cerocahui.

Wright's Snakeweed/*Gutierrezia wrightii*

Polymnia maculata

Yellow Daisy- and Dandelion-like

Mexican Zinnia, Creeping Zinnia
Zinnia angustifolia

• Aster family Asteraceae
Plant: 8–12" tall.
Flower: 1" wide.
Description: Small yellow daisy-like flower with 9 rays, pattern of yellow orange on outside of each ray, yellow on inside of each ray, small disk. Blooms on bushy, spreading, 1" linear leaves, opposite. Margins entire.
Habitat: Roadside, rocky, dry, sun. Elevation 4562'.
Range: Southeast U.S., Mexico.
Comments: Photographed in August on the roadside coming up out of the canyon from Urique.

• Familia del girasol Asteraceae
Planta: de 20–30 cm de alto.
Flor: de 2.5 cm de ancho.
Descripción: Pequeñas cabezuelas con 9 flores liguladas, de color Amarillo anaranjado por las afueras y Amarillo por dentro, flores tubulares pequeñas. Flores sostenidas por hojas opuestras de 2.5 cm de largo, márgenes enteros.
Hábitat: Orillas de camino, lugares pedregosos, secos y asoleados. Elevación 1390 m.
Distribución: Suroeste de USA y México.
Comentarios: Fotografiada en Agosto por el camino saliendo del canon de Urique.

Aster

• Aster family Asteraceae
Plant: 12" tall.
Flower: 1" wide.
Description: Yellow daisy-like flower, 8 rays rounded at the ends, slightly raised center. Leaves compound, 1" long, narrowly lanceolate, slightly toothed margins.
Habitat: Edge of pasture, loam, moist, sun. Elevation 5354'.
Range: Chihuahua, Mexico.
Comments: Photographed in August near Cerocahui after crossing the Arroyo del Cerocahui, in the field on the left before beginning the climb into the mountains.

• Familia Asteraceae
Planta: de 30 cm de alto.
Flor: de 2.5 cm de ancho.
Descripción: Cabezuela estrellada, amarilla, con 8 flores liguladas con el ápice redondo. Hojas compuestas, de 2.5 cm de largo, angostas, lanceoladas, ligeramente dentadas en los márgenes.
Hábitat: Orillas de los agostaderos, suelos francos, húmedos, asoleados. Elevación 1632 m.
Range: Chihuahua, México.
Comentarios: Fotografiada en agosto cerca de Cerocahui, después del cruce del Arroyo Cerocahui en el campo sobre la acera izquierda antes de la subida de la sierra.

Mexican Zinnia, Creeping Zinnia/*Zinnia angustifolia*

Aster

47

Yellow Daisy- and Dandelion-like

Orange Zexmenia
Wedelia hispida

• Aster family Asteraceae
Plant: Groundcover to 17" tall.
Flower: 3/4–1 1/4" wide.
Description: Yellow daisy-like flower, 9–13 ray flowers, central disk. Dark red woody stems. Leaves opposite, 1–2" long, lanceolate, margins toothed, rough hairs.
Habitat: Rocky slope, loam, dry, sun. Elevation 7021–7235'.
Range: Texas, Belize, Guatemala, Mexico.
Comments: Photographed in September on the road to Cerro Gallegos between basket cave (La Cueva) and fountain.

• Familia del girasol Asteraceae
Planta: Rastrera hasta 43 cm de alto.
Cabezuela: de 1.9 a 3.1 cm de ancho.
Descripción: Flor en Cabezuela provista de 9 a 13 flores liguladas, con flores tubulares en el centro. Tallos leñosos de color rojo oscuro. Hojas opuestas, de 2.5–5 cm de largo, lanceoladas, márgenes dentados, coriáceas.
Hábitat: Faldas rocosas. Suelos francos, secos, asoleados. Elevación 2140–2205 m.
Distribución: Texas, Belice, Guatemala, México.
Comentarios: Fotografiada en septiembre sobre el camino al Cerro Gallegos entre La Cueva y el manantial.

Not Yet Identified

• Aster family Asteraceae
Plant: 30–38" tall.
Flower: 1 3/4" wide.
Description: Yellow daisy-like flower, 8 distinctly separated ray flowers, 1/4" raised disk. Deeply lobed, compound leaves 2–2 1/2" long, margins entire.
Habitat: Side of access road, heavily forested, rocky with leaf debris, moist, shade. Elevation 5640'.
Range: Chihuahua, Mexico.
Comments: Photographed in September at Tascate–El Cajón trail on logging road, Cerocahui.

• Familia del girasol Asteraceae
Planta: de 76 a 97 cm de alto.
Flor: de 4.4 cm de ancho.
Descripción: Cabezuela con flores radialmente arregladas, con 8 flores liguladas bien separadas, flores tubulares de 6 mm de largo, salientes. Hojas profundamente lobuladas, compuestas de 5–6.3 cm de largo, márgenes enteros.
Hábitat: Orillas de camino, área boscosa, suelo rocoso con hojarasca, húmedo, sombreado. Elevación 1719 m.
Distribución: Chihuahua, México.
Comentarios: Fotografiada en septiembre sobre camino a Táscate–El Cajón, Cerocahui.

Orange Zexmenia/*Wedelia hispida*

Not Yet Identified

Yellow Daisy- and Dandelion-like

Mexican Coneflower
Ratibida mexicana

• Aster family Asteraceae
Plant: 24" tall.
Flower: 2 1/2" wide, disk 1" long.
Description: Yellow daisy-like flower, 9 ray flowers with 1" high flower head with yellow green disk flowers. Each ray 3/4" long, divided into 3 points at end. Leaves alternate, pinnately compound, 2 1/2–3" long. Margins toothed.
Habitat: Hillside on edge of valley, soil loam and broken up volcanic rock, dry, sun. Elevation 7652'.
Range: Chihuahua, Coahuila, and Durango in Mexico.
Comments: Photographed in September after the right hand turn into San Ignacio valle, 2.5 miles from Creel.

• Familia del girasol Asteraceae
Planta: de 60 cm de alto.
Cabezuela: de 6.3 cm de ancho, flor tubular de 2.5 cm de largo.
Descripción: Cabezuela en forma radial, amarilla, 9 flores liguladas arregladas sobre una Cabezuela de 2.5 cm de largo, con flores tubulares de color verde-amarillo. Cada flor ligulada de 1.9 cm de largo, pétalo dividido en 3 en el ápice. Hojas alternas, compuestas pinnadamente de 6.3–7.5 cm de largo, márgenes dentados.
Hábitat: Lomeríos, suelo franco y roca volcanica, seco, asoleado. Elevación 2332 m.
Distribución: Chihuahua, Coahuila y Durango en México.
Comentarios: Fotografiada en septiembre después de la vuelta a la derecha al Valle de San Ignacio, 4 km de Creel.

Not Yet Identified

• Aster family Asteraceae
Plant: 25" tall.
Flower: 3 1/4" wide.
Description: Yellow daisy-like flower, with 7 ray flowers on single stem, orange disk, loved by butterflies. Leaves arranged 3 opposite, 1 1/2" long, small lanceolate, several leaves on side branches, margins toothed.
Habitat: Large rocks on top of rock cliff, loam, dry, sun. Elevation 5446'.
Range: Chihuahua, Mexico.
Comments: Photographed in August on rock cliffs above Paraiso del Oso, near Cerocahui.

• Familia del girasol Asteraceae
Planta: de 63.5 cm de alto.
Flor: de 7.8 cm de ancho.
Descripción: Cabezuela estrellada, amarilla, con 7 flores liguladas sobre un solo tallo, las flores tubulares anaranjadas, buscadas por las mariposas. Hojas opuestas, a veces 3 en el nudo, de 3.8 cm de largo, pequeñas, lanceoladas, numerosas, márgenes dentados.
Hábitat: Sobre piedras grandes del alcantarillado, suelo franco, seco, asoleado. Elevación 1660 m.
Distribución: Chihuahua, México.
Comentarios: Fotografiada en agosto sobre alcantarillado rocoso arriba de Paraiso del Oso, cerca de Cerocahui.

Mexican Coneflower/*Ratibida mexicana*

Not Yet Identified

Yellow Daisy- and Dandelion-like

Fivenerve Helianthella
Helianthella quinquenervis

• Aster family Asteraceae
Plant: 21" tall.
Flower: 5" wide.
Description: Yellow daisy-like flower, 18 ray flowers. Disk flowers are yellow, 1 1/2" across. Stem hairy. Leaves opposite and alternate, lanceolate with prominent veins, 3 1/2–9 1/2" long. Margins entire. Roots have strong odor.
Habitat: Edge of valley, soil loam with broken up volcanic rock, dry, sun. Elevation 7652'.
Range: Arizona, Colorado, Idaho, Montana, New Mexico, Nevada, Oregon, South Dakota, Utah, Wyoming, Chihuahua and Nuevo León in Mexico.
Comments: Photographed in September after the right hand turn into San Ignacio valle, 2.5 miles from Creel.

• Familia del girasol Asteraceae
Planta: de 53 cm de alto.
Cabezuela: de 12.5 cm de ancho.
Descripción: Cabezuela radialmente simétrica, amarilla con 18 flores liguladas, flores tubulares amarillas, de 3.8 cm de ancho. Tallos peludos. Hojas opuestas y alternas, lanceoladas con nervaduras visibles, de 8.8–23.8 cm de largo, márgenes enteros. Las raíces tienen un olor muy fuerte.
Hábitat: Lomeríos, suelo franco y roca volcanica, seco, asoleado. Elevación 2332 m.
Distribución: Arizona, Colorado, Idaho, Montana, Nuevo Mexico, Nevada, Oregon, Dakota de Sur, Utah, Wyoming, Chihuahua y Nuevo Leon en México.
Comentarios: Fotografiada en septiembre después de la vuelta a la derecha al Valle de San Ignacio, 4 km de Creel.

Yellow Bilaterally Symmetrical

Mexican Squawroot
Conopholis mexicana

• Broomrape family Orobanchaceae
Plant: 4–12" tall.
Description: Pale yellow erect club-like stems. Numerous curved bilaterally symmetrical flowers. Lower stem has pale yellow leaves that lack chlorophyll. This plant is a parasitic flowering plant that lives on decaying leaves.
Habitat: Loam under trees.
Range: Arizona, Colorado, New Mexico, Texas, Mexico.
Comments: This plant was sighted and photographed in the spring by Bonnie Dirk. This plant has not been verified for accuracy of identification.

• Familia Orobanchaceae
Planta: de 10– 30 cm de alto.
Descripción: Tallos erectos, amarillentos. Numerosas flores bilateralmente simétricas. Hojas básales carentes de clorofila. Esta planta es una parasita que crece sobre hojas muertas.
Hábitat: Sobre suelo franco debajo de los árboles.
Distribución: Arizona, Colorado, Nuevo Mexico, Texas, México.
Comentarios: Encontrada y fotografiada en la primavera por Bonnie Dirk. La precisión de la identificación de esta planta no ha sido verificada.

Fivenerve Helianthella/*Helianthella quinquenervis*

Mexican Squawroot/*Conopholis mexicana*

Yellow Bilaterally Symmetrical

Smooththroat Stoneseed, Smooth Pucoon
Lithospermum cobrense

• Borage family Boraginaceae
Plant: 14" tall.
Flower: 1/2" long, 1/2" wide.
Description: Pale yellow bilaterally symmetrical flower with 1/4" long tube then flair of 5 united petals, small brown stamens. Multiple blossoms on end of stems. Stem hairy, erect. Leaves alternate, linear, hairy, 1/2–1" long. Margins entire.
Habitat: River bed, soil rocky, moist, sun. Elevation 7308'.
Range: Arizona, New Mexico, Texas, Mexico.
Comments: Photographed in September at Choquita, 5 miles from Creel.

• Familia Boraginaceae
Planta: de 35.5 cm de alto.
Flor: de 1.3 cm de largo, por 1.3 cm de ancho.
Descripción: Flores amarillas, bilateralmente simétricas sobre un tubo de 6 mm de largo, terminando con 5 pétalos unidos, estambres pequeños, cafés. Tallos terminando con muchas flores, erectos, peludos; hojas alternas, lineares, peludas, de 1.3–2.5 cm de largo, márgenes enteros.
Hábitat: Orillas de ríos, suelo rocoso, húmedo, asoleado. Elevación 2227 m.
Distribución: Arizona, Nuevo México, Texas, México.
Comentarios: Fotografiada en septiembre en Choguita, 8 km de Creel.

Amicia zygomeris

• Pea family Fabaceae
Plant: 30–40" tall.
Flower: 1 1/2" long, 7/8" wide.
Description: Yellow bilaterally symmetrical flower. Leaves palmately compound, alternate, 1 1/2" x 1 1/2", heart shaped, margins entire.
Habitat: Side of river creek, moist, sand, semi-shade. Elevation 5432'.
Range: Mexico.
Comments: Photographed in September along Arroyo de El Cajón, Cerocahui.

• Familia del frijol Fabaceae
Planta: de 76–102 cm de alto.
Flor: de 3.8 cm de largo, por 2.2 cm de ancho.
Descripción: Flores amarillas, bilateralmente simétricas. Hojas palmeadamente compuestas, alternas, de 3.8 x 3.8 cm, en forma de corazón, márgenes enteros.
Hábitat: Orillas de arroyos, húmedos, arenosos, semi sombreados. Elevación 1656 m.
Distribución: México.
Comentarios: Fotografiada en septiembre a lo largo del Arroyo de El Cajón, Cerocahui.

Smooththroat Stoneseed, Smooth Pucoon/
Lithospermum cobrense

Amicia zygomeris

Yellow Bilaterally Symmetrical

Senna pallida
- Pea family Fabaceae
Plant: 30–40" tall.
Flower: 3/4" long, 1 1/4" wide.
Description: Yellow shrub-like plant, bilaterally symmetrical, 5 petals—3 larger ones that curl upward, 2 smaller ones, prominent green pistil, thick stamen. Leaves alternate, pinnately compound, 1/2–1" long. Margins entire.
Habitat: Rocky trail through creek bed, rock and sand, damp, sun. Elevation 2170'.
Range: Grenada, El Salvador, Mexico.
Comments: Photographed in September in Arroyo Los Tachos, Batopilas.

- Familia del frijol Fabaceae
Planta: de 76 a 102 cm de alto.
Flor: de 1.9 cm de largo, por 3.1 cm de ancho.
Descripción: Planta arbustiva, con flor amarilla, bilateralmente simétrica, con 5 pétalos: 3 grandes doblados hacia arriba, y 2 más pequeños, un pistilo verde prominente, estambres gruesos. Hojas alternas, pinnadamente compuestas, de 1.3 a 2.5 cm de largo, márgenes enteros.
Hábitat: Camino rocoso a lo largo del arroyo, suelo arenoso, húmedo, asoleado. Elevación 661 m.
Distribución: Grenada, El Salvador, México.
Comentarios: Fotografiada en septiembre en Arroyo Los Tachos, Batopilas.

Trumpetbush, Esperanza
Tecoma stans
- Trumpet creeper family Bignoniaceae
Shrub: 10–15' tall.
Flower: 2 3/4" long, 1 1/2" wide.
Description: Large yellow shrub, multi-branching, clusters of bilaterally symmetrical trumpet-shaped flowers, 5 lobes; 2 smaller on top, 3 larger ones on bottom; 3 red stripes leading into throat, buds have red tinge on outside. Leaves opposite, linear, 1 1/2–2 3/4" long. Margins occasionally toothed. According to Robert Vine, this shrub was used by the Indian and Mexican peoples of the southwest and Mexico for bow making, bee fodder, and medicines.
Habitat: Along road, rock cut back, rocks and sand, arid, sun. Elevation 4350'.
Range: Native to South and Central America, north to Mexico and the southwestern U.S.
Comments: Photographed in September on the road to San Ignacio, 5 miles from Batopilas, Rebenton.

- Familia Bignoniaceae
Arbusto: de 3-4.5 m de alto.
Flor: de 6.9 cm de largo, por 3.8 cm de ancho.
Descripción: Arbusto grande, muy ramificado, con flores amarillas, bilateralmente simétricas, en forma de trompeta, pétalos unidos terminando en 5 lobulos: 2 labios grandes superiores y 3 inferiores más pequeños; 3 rallas rojas en la garganta de la corola. Hojas opuestas, lineares, de 1.3 a 6.9 cm de largo, márgenes a veces detados. Según Robert Vine, este arbusto fue usado por los indios y la gente mexicana del suroeste y de Mexico para hacer arcos y medicina.
Hábitat: A lo largo del camino, suelo rocoso, arenoso, seco, asoleado. Elevación 1326 m.
Distribución: Nativo del sur y centro America, norte de México y suroeste de de USA.
Comentarios: Fotografiada en septiembre sobre camino a San Ignacio, 8 km de Batopilas, Rebenton.

Senna pallida

Trumpetbush, Esperanza/*Tecoma stans*

Yellow Elongated Clusters

Torrey's Craglily
Echeandia flavescens

• Lily family Liliaceae
Plant: 10–12" tall.
Flower: 3/4" wide.
Description: Yellow elongated cluster, radially symmetrical flower with 6 petals (3 smaller, 3 larger), 6 stamens and stigma protruding out of center. Thin grasslike basal leaves 4 1/2" long.
Habitat: Volcanic plateau growing between rocks, moist, rocky, sun. Elevation 5665'.
Range: Arizona, New Mexico, Texas, Mexico.
Comments: Photographed in September on a volcanic plateau in between Cave of Crosses and Cave of Skull, Cerocahui.

• Familia Liliaceae
Planta: de 25.4–30 cm de alto.
Flor: de 1.9 cm de ancho.
Descripción: Flor amarilla, radialmente simétrica con 6 pétalos (tépalos): 3 grandes y 3 pequeños; 6 estambres y el estigma saliente del centro. Hojas delgadas, lineares, básales, de 11.5 cm de largo.
Hábitat: Mesa volcánica, rocosa, húmedo, asoleado. Elevación 1727 m.
Distribución: Arizona, Nuevo México, Texas, México.
Comentarios: Fotografiada en septiembre sobre una mesa volcánica entre la Cueva de las Cruces y la Cueva del Cráneo, Cerocahui.

Yellow Rounded Clusters

Seemann Groundsel, Geranio del Campo
Senecio carlomasonii

• Aster family Asteraceae
Plant: 27–39" tall.
Flower: 1/4" wide.
Description: Yellow rounded cluster of radially symmetrical flowers, 5–6 petals. Spotted stem. Alternate, round, toothed leaves 2–3 3/4" long. Margins toothed.
Habitat: Up from stream bed, rocky sand, moist, sun. Elevation 5454'.
Range: Southern Arizona and Sonora, Chihuahua, Nayarit in Mexico.
Comments: Photographed in September on the trail to Cave of Crosses near Paraiso del Oso, Cerocahui.

• Familia del girasol Asteraceae
Planta: de 69 a 99 cm de alto.
Cabezuela: de 6 mm de ancho.
Descripción: Flores amarillas arregladas radialmente en una cabezuela, de 5 a 6 flores liguladas. Tallos pecosos. Hojas alternas, redondas, dentadas, de 5 a 9.4 cm de largo, con márgenes dentados.
Hábitat: Orillas de arroyo, arena pedregosa, humeda, asoleada. Elevación 1662 m.
Distribución: Sur de Arizona y Sonora, Chihuahua, Nayarit en México.
Comentarios: Fotografiada en septiembre sobre caminos a la Cueva de las Cruces cerca de Paraiso del Oso, Cerocahui.

Torrey's Craglily/*Echeandia flavescens*

Seemann Groundsel, Geranio del Campo/
Senecio carlomasonii

Yellow Rounded Clusters

Hymenopappus palmeri

- Aster family Asteraceae
Plant: 27–30" tall.
Flower: 1/4" wide.
Description: Yellow rounded cluster of flowers, disks 1/4" wide with no obvious petals. Alternate, compound spiky leaves 1–2" long.
Habitat: Up from stream bed, sand and rocks, moist, semi-shade. Elevation 5471'.
Range: Chihuahua and Durango, Mexico.
Comments: Photographed in September at Tascate along the stream near Paraiso del Oso, Cerocahui.

- Familia del girasol Asteraceae
Planta: de 69 a 76 cm de alto.
Cabezuela: de 6 mm de ancho.
Descripción: Flores amarillas, agrupadas en Cabezuela, flores tubulares de 6 mm de ancho, sin presencia aparente de flores liguladas. Hojas alternas, compuestas, dentadas, de 2.5 a 5 cm de largo.
Hábitat: Orillas de arroyo, arena pedregosa, humeda, semi-asoleada. Elevación 1668 m.
Distribución: Chihuahua y Durango, México.
Comentarios: Fotografiada en septiembre en Táscate a lo largo del arroyo cerca de Paraiso del Oso, Cerocahui.

Not Yet Identified

- Aster family Asteraceae
Plant: 12" tall.
Flower: head 3/8" wide.
Description: Yellow rounded cluster of rayless flower heads. Alternate, elliptic, toothed leaves 1–1 3/4" long. Margins toothed.
Habitat: Meadow, rock and sand, dry, sun. Elevation 5360'.
Range: Chihuahua, Mexico.
Comments: Photographed in September near Tascate, Cerocahui.

- Familia del girasol Asteraceae
Planta: de 30 cm de alto.
Cabezuela: de 9 mm de ancho.
Descripción: Flores amarillas agrupadas en Cabezuela sin flores liguladas. Hojas alternas, elípticas, dentadas, de 2.5 a 4.4 cm de largo, márgenes dentados.
Hábitat: Llanos, suelo rocoso y arenoso, seco, asoleado. Elevación 1634 m.
Distribución: Chihuahua, México.
Comentarios: Fotografiada en septiembre cerca de Táscate, Cerocachui.

Hymenopappus palmeri

Not Yet Identified

Yellow Rounded Clusters

Galactia

• Pea family Fabaceae
Plant: 11" tall.
Flower: 1 1/2" wide.
Description: Yellow rounded clusters of bilaterally symmetrical flowers. Leaves alternate, 1–3" long, lanceolate, margins entire.
Habitat: Volcanic rock, loam, moist, semi-shade. Elevation 5462'.
Range: Chihuahua, Mexico.
Comments: Photographed in August behind Paraiso del Oso above Arroyo del Ranchito, near Cerocahui.

• Familia del frijol Fabaceae
Planta: de 28 cm de alto.
Flor: de 3.8 cm de ancho.
Descripción: Flores aglomeradas, amarillas, bilateralmente simétricas. Hojas alternas, 2.5–7.5 cm de largo, lanceoladas, márgenes enteros.
Hábitat: Rocas volcánicas, francos, húmedos, semí-asoleados. Elevación 1665 m.
Distribución: Chihuahua, México.
Comentarios: Fotografiada en agosto detrás de Paraiso del Oso, arriba del Arroyo del Ranchito, cerca de Cerocahui.

Galactia

Part Three Orange Flowers

Orange Radially Symmetrical

Mexican Catchfly, Indian Pink
Silene laciniata

• Pink family Caryophyllaceae
Plant: 12–16" tall.
Flower: 1 1/4–1 1/2" wide.
Description: Red orange radially symmetrical flower, opens out flat into 5 petal-like lobes, each lobe is deeply cut, whitish ring at the center, prominent stamens, 1 1/2" long orange green calyx. Leaves opposite, linear, 1 1/4–2" long. Margins entire.
Habitat: Rocky cliff by road where it has been cut out, dry, semi-shade. Elevation 7070'.
Range: New Mexico, Texas, Arizona, California, and Chihuahua in Mexico.
Comments: Photographed in September on the road from Guachochi to Tónachi, 5.5 miles to left hand turn to Tónachi, then 11.9 miles.

• Familia Caryophyllaceae
Planta: de 30 a 41 cm de alto.
Flor: de 3.1 a 3.8 cm de ancho.
Descripción: Flor roja anaranjada radialmente simétrica, abriendo en 5 segmentos parecidos a pétalos, cada segmento cortado profundamente, con un anillo blanquecino en el centro, estambres prominentes de 3.8 cm de largo, cáliz largo verde anaranjado. Hojas opuestas, lineares de 3.1 a 5 cm de largo, márgenes enteros.
Hábitat: Acantilados rocosos sobre orillas de camino, seco, semi sombreado. Elevación 2155 m.
Distribución: Nuevo México, Texas, Arizona, California, Chihuahua en México.
Comentarios: Fotografiada en septiembre sobre camino de Guachochi a Tónachi, 9 km a la izquiera a Tónachi, después 19 km.

Red Dahlia
Dahlia coccinea

• Aster family Asteraceae
Plant: 20–28" tall.
Flower: 2" wide.
Description: Red orange radially symmetrical flower, 8 ray flowers, 1/2" high yellow disk. Trifoliate, compound leaves 1 1/2–2" long. Margins toothed. Tubers. Visited by hummingbirds.
Habitat: Side of trail, rocky incline, damp, sun. Elevation 5670'.
Range: District of Columbia, U.S., Guatemala, and Durango, Sinaloa, Chihuahua in Mexico.
Comments: Photographed in September at Tascate, El Cajón trail on logging road, Cerocahui.

• Familia del girasol Asteraceae
Planta: de 50 a 71 cm de alto.
Cabezuela: de 5 cm de ancho.
Descripción: Flores rojo anaranjadas radialmente simétricas y arregladas en Cabezuela con 8 flores liguladas, y flores tubulares de 1.3 cm de largo. Hojas compuestas, trifoliadas de 3.8 a 5 cm de largo, márgenes dentados. Raíces tuberculosas. Las flores son visitadas frecuentemente por colibrí.
Hábitat: Orillas de camino, rocoso, húmedo, asoleado. Elevación 1728 m.
Distribución: Distrito de Colombia, U.S.A., Guatemala, y Durango, Sinaloa, Chihuahua en México.
Comentarios: Fotografiada en septiembre en Táscate, camino al Cajón, Cerocahui.

Mexican Catchfly, Indian Pink/*Silene laciniata*

Red Dahlia/*Dahlia coccinea*

Orange Radially Symmetrical

Trans-Pecos Indian Paintbrush
Castilleja nervata

• Figwort family Scrophulariaceae
Plant: 10" tall.
Description: Red orange radially symmetrical leaf bracts grow around upper 2 1/4" of stem. Bracts go from green to red/orange. Leaves alternate, linear, 1–2" long. Margins entire with hairs.
Habitat: Along road on rocky cliff, rock and sand, dry, sun. Elevation 6800'.
Range: Arizona and Coahuila, Durango, Jalisco, Nayarit, Chihuahua in Mexico.
Comments: Photographed in September on the road to Batopilas, km marker 12.8 from paved road.

• Familia Scrophulariaceae
Planta: de 25.4 cm de alto
Descripción: Flores rojo anaranjadas radialemente simétricas sostenidas por bracteas foliares, terminales ocupando los 5.7 cm del tallo. Las bracteas van desde verdes a rojo anaranjadas. Hojas alternas, lineares, de 2.5 a 5 cm de largo, márgenes enteros, ciliados.
Hábitat: A lo largo del camino sobre pendiente rocosa, suelo rocoso y arenoso, seco, asoleado. Elevación 2073 m.
Distribución: Arizona, y Coahuila, Durango, Jalisco, Nayarit, Chihuahua en México.
Comentarios: Fotografiada en septiembre sobre camino a Batopilas, marcador de km 12.8, camino pavimentado.

Orange Bilaterally Symmetrical

Phaseolus

• Pea family Fabaceae
Plant: 6 1/2" tall.
Flower: 1 1/2" long.
Description: Apricot bilaterally symmetrical flower, 2 petals and small yellow center. One compound leaf at base, 1" long, slightly lanceolate with rounded point, leaf has 3 leaflets—2 lower with notch in them. Margins entire.
Habitat: Top of hillside, sand and red clay, moist, sun. Elevation 5673'.
Range: Chihuahua, Mexico.
Comments: Photographed in August off the east side of the road between Paraiso del Oso and Bahuichivo, near Cerocahui.

• Familia del frijol Fabaceae
Planta: de 16.3 cm de alto.
Flor: de 3.8 cm de largo.
Descripción: Flores bilateralmente simétricas, 2 pétalos y un pequeño centro amarillo. Hojas compuestas de 2.5 cm de largo, ligeramente lanceoladas con puntas redondas, trifoliadas, los 2 foliolos más abajo con ápice ligeramente hendido, márgenes enteros.
Hábitat: Arriba de la loma, suelo arenoso y arcilloso de color rojo, húmedo, asoleado. Elevación 1729 m.
Distribución: Chihuahua, México.
Comentarios: Fotografiada en agosto sobre el lado este del camino entre Paraiso del Oso y Bahuichivo, cerca de Cerocahui.

Trans-Pecos Indian Paintbrush/*Castilleja nervata*

Phaseolus

Orange Bilaterally Symmetrical

Mexican Shell Flower
Trigridia pavonia

- Iris family Iridaceae

Plant: 11" tall.

Flower: 3" wide.

Description: Orange bilaterally symmetrical flower, 3 petals, each 1 1/2" long, on outside, a "tigerish" pattern of orange, yellow, and white inside the cup, layered by 3 interconnecting circles pointed on one end, one 2" pistil. Three 5–7 1/2" swordlike linear leaves, margins entire. Bulb.

Habitat: Loam, moist, semi-shade. Elevation 6938'.

Range: Mexico, South America.

Comments: Photographed in September in the garden of a local naturalist, on road to Cerro Gallegos.

- Familia Iridaceae

Planta: de 27.9 cm de alto.

Flor: de 7.5 cm de ancho.

Descripción: Flores anaranjadas bilateralmente simétricas, 3 pétalos de 3.8 cm de largo cada uno, por las afueras pintados de amarillo con el color de la piel de tigre y blancos por dentro, con capas de 3 círculos que interconectan y apuntando hacia un extremo, un estigma de 5 cm de largo. Tres hojas lanceoladas, lineares de 12.5 a 18.8 cm de largo, márgenes enteros. Raíces bulbosas.

Hábitat: Suelo franco, húmedo, semi-sombreado. Elevación 2115 m.

Distribución: México, Sur America.

Comentarios: Fotografiada en septiembre en el jardín de un local naturista, camino a Cerro Gallegos.

Orange Elongated Clusters

Castilleja stenophylla

- Figwort family Scrophulariaceae

Plant: 5" tall.

Flower: 3/4" long, 1/8" wide.

Description: Red orange elongated cluster with bilaterally symmetrical tubular petals. Petals open with longer green/yellow protrusions, looks like flames. Alternate, very narrow linear leaves 1/2–3/4" long. Margins entire.

Habitat: Open field, soil hard packed sandy loam, dry, sun. Elevation 7641'.

Range: Chihuahua and Durango, Mexico.

Comments: Photographed in September after the left hand turn into San Ignacio, 4.5 miles from Creel.

- Familia Scrophulariaceae

Planta: de 12.5 cm de alto.

Flor: de 1.9 cm de largo, por 3 mm de ancho.

Descripción: Flores agrupadas, elongadas, rojo anaranjadas, con pétalos tubulares, bilateralmente simétricos. Pétalos incrustados de lineas longitudinales de verde amarillo, parecido a una flama. Hojas alternas, muy angostas, lineares, de 1.3 a 1.9 cm, márgenes enteros.

Hábitat: Llano, suelo compacto, franco-arenoso, seco, asoleado. Elevación 2329 m.

Distribución: Chihuahua y Durango, México.

Comentarios: Fotografiada en septiembre después de la vuelta a la izquierda hacia San Ignacio, 7.7 km de Creel.

Mexican Shell Flower/*Trigridia pavonia*

Castilleja stenophylla

Orange Elongated Clusters

Santa Catalina Indian Paintbrush
Castilleja tenuiflora

- Figwort family Scrophulariaceae
Plant: 20–24" tall.
Flower: 3/4–1 1/4" long, 1/8" wide.
Description: Red orange elongated cluster, opens with longer yellow petal that splits open, 3 black seeds at base, looks like flames, long stamens full length of yellow petal. Woody stem. Alternate, pointed linear leaves 1/4–1 1/2" long, margins entire.
Habitat: Side of road, rocky shear cliff, moist, sun. Elevation 7021'.
Range: Texas, New Mexico, Arizona, Mexico.
Comments: Photographed in September on the road to Cerro Gallegos near La Cueva (basket cave).

- Familia Scrophulariaceae
Planta: de 50 a 60 cm de alto.
Flor: de 1.9 a 3.1 cm de largo, por 3 mm de ancho.
Descripción: Flores rojo anaranjadas, agrupadas, abiertas con un pétalo más largo y dividido, 3 semillas negras en la base, parecido a flamas, estambres largos casi del tamaño del pétalo. Tallo leñoso. Hojas alternas, puntiagudas, lineares, de 6 mm a 3.8 cm de largo, márgenes enteros.
Hábitat: Orillas de camino, pendiente rocosa, húmeda, asoleado. Elevación 2140 m.
Distribución: Texas, Nuevo México, Arizona, México.
Comentarios: Fotografiada en septiembre sobre camino a Cerro Gallegos, cerca de la Cueva.

Huachuca Indian Paintbrush
Castilleja patriotica

- Figwort family Scrophulariaceae
Plant: 18" tall.
Flower: 1 1/2" long, 1/4" wide.
Description: Red/orange/yellow-green elongated cluster. Each colored flower bract is orange on outer half, lime green on lower half. Each bract projects from stem at an angle, center lobes protrude out of bract and splits underneath. Leaves alternate, divided into 3–5 narrow lobes, 1/2–3/4" long. Margins entire.
Habitat: Hillside on edge of valley, soil loam with broken up volcanic rock, dry, sun. Elevation 7652'.
Range: Arizona, New Mexico, Chihuahua and Durango in Mexico.
Comments: Photographed in September after the right hand turn into San Ignacio valle, 2.5 miles from Creel.

- Familia Scrophulariaceae
Planta: de 45 cm de alto.
Flor: de 3.8 cm de largo, por 6 mm de ancho.
Descripción: Flores rojas, anaranjadas, amarillo-verduscas, agrupadas, terminales. Cada bráctea coloreada de la flor es anaranjada en la mitad exterior y verde limón en la otra mitad. Cada bráctea sale del tallo en un ángulo, los lóbulos centrales sobresalen las brácteas y se dividen en la base. Hojas alternas, divididas en 3–5 lóbulos angostos, de 1.3 a 1.9 cm de largo, márgenes enteros.
Hábitat: Lomas sobre orillas del valle, suelo franco con roca volcanica quebrada, seco, asoleado. Elevación 2332 m.
Distribución: Arizona, Nuevo México, Chihuahua y Durango en México.
Comentarios: Fotografiada en septiembre después de la vuelta a la izquierda hacia el valle de San Ignacio, 4 km de Creel.

Santa Catalina Indian Paintbrush/*Castilleja tenuiflora*

Huachuca Indian Paintbrush/*Castilleja patriotica*

Orange Elongated Clusters

Penstemon wislizeni

- Figwort family Scrophulariaceae
Plant: 25" tall.
Flower: 1 1/4" long, 1/4" wide.
Description: Orange red elongated cluster with bilaterally symmetrical 2 lipped tubular flowers—2 lobed upper, 3 lobed lower—stamens inside upper, white beard around edge of flower, 1/4" calyx holding tubular flower. Multi-stemmed, 3/16" thick, green on one side, maroon on other. Leaves opposite, linear, 3–4" long. Margins entire.
Habitat: River bed, soil rocky, moist, sun. Elevation 7308'.
Range: Chihuahua, Durango, Sinaloa, Puebla, and Nuevo León in Mexico.
Comments: Photographed in September at Choquita, 5 miles from Creel.

- Familia Scrophulariaceae
Planta: de 63.5 cm de alto.
Flor: de 3.1 cm de largo, por 6 mm de ancho.
Descripción: Flores anaranjado rojas, agrupadas, con una corola tubular bilateralmente simétrica con 2 labios superiores y 3 inferiores, estambres adentro de los labios superiores, vellosidades blancas en la boca del tubo de la flor, cáliz de 6 mm de largo sosteniendo el tubo en la base. Tallos numerosos, de 4.5 mm de grueso, verdes en un lado y morados en el otro. Hojas opuestas, lineares, de 7.5 a 10 cm de largo. Márgenes enteros.
Hábitat: Lecho del río, suelo rocoso, húmedo, asoleado. Elevación 2227 m.
Distribución: Chihuahua, Durango, Sinaloa, Puebla y Nuevo León en México.
Comentarios: Fotografiada en septiembre en Choguita, 8 km de Creel.

Woolly Senna

Senna hirsuta

- Pea family Fabaceae
Plant: Shrub 3'–6' tall.
Flower: 1/2" long, 1/2" wide.
Description: Shrub has elongated flower clusters with 2–8 tangerine flowers arranged along central stem on top 9" of shrub. Leaves alternate on stem, opposite on branches, ovate, 1 1/2" long, margins entire.
Habitat: Roadside, sun. Elevation 4953'.
Range: Southwest U.S., Mexico, Central and South America.
Comments: Photographed in August on the road coming up out of the canyon from Urique.

- Familia del frijol Fabaceae
Planta: de 0.9 a 1.8 m de alto.
Flor: de 1.3 cm de largo, por 1.3 cm de ancho.
Descripción: Arbusto con una inflorescencia alargada con 2–8 flores, anaranjadas, arregladas sobre un eje central en la porción terminal del arbusto. Hojas alternas en el tallo, opuestas en las ramas, ovadas, de 3.8 cm de largo, márgenes enteros.
Hábitat: A lo largo del camino, asoleado. Elevación 1510 m.
Distribución: Suroeste de USA, México, Centro y Sur América.
Comentarios: Fotografiada en agosto sobre saliendo del cañón de Urique.

Penstemon wislizeni

Woolly Senna/*Senna hirsuta*

Orange Elongated Clusters

Jarritas
Stenorrhynchus aurantiacus

• Orchid family Orchidaceae
Plant: 22" tall.
Flower: 1 3/4" long.
Description: Orange elongated clusters of tubular flowers 1/2" wide, 1 3/4" long, brown dots radiate at top from central stem. Bluish green 4–5" perfoliate lanceolate leaves spread out at bottom, then are tight to stem up to flower. Leaf margins entire.
Habitat: On volcanic ryolitic tuff rock slope above stream, loam, dry, sun. Elevation 5433'.
Range: Mexico and Guatemala.
Comments: Photographed in August across the road from Paraiso del Oso on rocks above Arroyo del Tortuga, Cerocahui.

• Familia Orchidaceae
Planta: de 56 cm de alto.
Flor: de 4.4 cm de largo.
Descripción: Inflorescencias de flores anaranjadas y tubulares sobre ramas terminales, alargadas, de 1.3 cm de ancho, 4.4 cm de largo, puntos cafés sobre porción superior del tallo. Hojas perfoliadas, extendiéndose en la base, después adheridas al tallo en la parte superior, azul-verdes, de 10 a 12.5 cm de largo, márgenes enteros.
Hábitat: Sobre pendiente de roca riolitica volcánica arriba del arroyo, suelo franco, seco, asoleado. Elevación 1656 m.
Distribución: México y Guatemala.
Comentarios: Fotografiada en agosto cruzando el camino de Paraiso del Oso sobre rocas arriba del Arroyo Tortuga, Cerocahui.

Not Yet Identified

Description: Elongated cluster of long pointed orange blossoms on arching flower stalks. Stiff blade-like leaves with hairs on margins.
Habitat: Rocky ledge.
Range: Chihuahua, Mexico.
Comments: Sighted and photographed in the spring by Bonnie Dirk off the side of the trail to Tortuga high vista, near Paraiso del Oso, Cerocahui.

Descripción: Inflorescencia alargada, terminal, con flores anaranjadas. Hojas con laminas rígidas y ciliadas en los márgenes.
Hábitat: Orillas rocosas.
Distribución: Chihuahua, México.
Comentarios: Fotografiada en la primavera por Bonnie Dirk a un lado de la brecha a Tortuga Vista alta, cerca de Paraiso del Oso, Cerocahui.

arritas/*Stenorrhynchus aurantiacus*

Not Yet Identified

Orange Rounded Clusters

Sida ciliaris

- Mallow family Malvaceae
Plant: 6–10" tall.
Flower: 3/8" wide.
Description: Peach rounded cluster, radially symmetrical, 5 petals, red stripes radiating from center. Cluster surrounded by calyx with radiating leaves. Leaves opposite and alternate, linear, 1/2–1" long. Margins slightly toothed.
Habitat: Along trail in rocky area, sandy, wet, sun. Elevation 2050'.
Range: Hawaii, Texas, Florida, Puerto Rico, Virgin Islands, Mexico.
Comments: Photographed in September in Arroyo Los Tachos, Batopilas.

- Familia del algodón Malvaceae
Planta: de 15 a 25.4 cm de alto.
Flor: de 9 mm de ancho.
Descripción: Inflorescencia formada por flores radialmente simétricas, color durazno, 5 pétalos con rayas rojas saliendo del centro. Cáliz sostenido por brácteas foliáceas. Hojas opuestas y alternas, lineares, de 1.3 a 2.5 cm de largo, márgenes, ligeramente dentados.
Hábitat: A lo largo de la brecha en un lugar rocoso, arenoso, húmedo, asoleado. Elevación 625 m.
Distribución: Hawaii, Florida, Puerto Rico, Islas Vírgenes, México.
Comentarios: Fotografiada en septiembre en Arroyo Los Tachos, Batopilas.

Mexican Bird-of-Paradise, Tabachín
Caesalpinia pulcherrima

- Pea family Fabaceae
Plant: Shrub 3' tall.
Flower: 1 1/2" wide.
Description: Round clusters of tangerine and variegated red orange radially symmetrical flowers, 2" long bright red, conspicuous stamens that extend beyond the lobes. Each flower has 5 sepals, lower one large, hoodlike. Stems have alternate bipinnately compound leaves, oblong to ovate leaflets 1/2–1" long.
Habitat: Roadside, sun. Elevation 2560'.
Range: Sonoran deserts, Florida, Texas, West Indies, and Chihuahua, Mexico.
Comment: Photographed in August on the road coming out of the canyon from Urique.

- Familia del frijol Fabaceae
Arbusto: de 90 cm de alto.
Flor: de 1.3 cm de ancho.
Descripción: Inflorescencia formada por flores radialmente simétricas de color rojo anaranjado, estambres de 5 cm de largo, rojo claro, sobresaliendo de la flor. Cada flor tiene 5 sépalos, el que está más abajo de mas bajo ganchudo. Tallos tienen hojas compuestas bipinnadas, foliolos oblongos a ovados, de 1.3 a 2.5 cm de largo.
Hábitat: Orillas de camino, asoleado. Elevación 780 m.
Distribución: Desierto sonorense, Florida, Texas, Oceanía y Chihuahua, México.
Comentarios: Fotografiada en agosto sobre camino saliendo del cañón de Urique.

Sida ciliaris

Mexican Bird-of-Paradise, Tabachín/
Caesalpinia pulcherrima

Part Four Red Flowers

Red Radially Symmetrical

Scarlet Creeper, Transpecos Morning Glory
Ipomoea cristulata

• Morning glory family Convolvulaceae
Plant: Vine.
Flower: 1" long, 5/8" wide.
Description: Twining vine of red radially symmetrical trumpet shaped flowers, 5 lobes of united petals. Palmate deeply 3–5 lobed leaves, 2" x 2", margins entire, all from one side. Attracts hummingbirds.
Habitat: Side of river creek, moist, sand, semi-shade. Elevation 5432'.
Range: Kansas, South Carolina, Arizona, New Mexico, Texas, Mexico.
Comments: Photographed in September along the bank of Arroyo de El Cajón at Tascate, Cerocahui.

• Familia de la jicama Convolvulaceae
Planta: Trepadora.
Flor: de 2.5 cm de largo, por 1.6 cm de ancho.
Descripción: Una trepadora con flores rojas, radialmente simétricas, en forma de trompeta, pétalos unidos con 5 lóbulos. Hojas palmeadamente divididas en 3–5 lóbulos, de 5 cm x 5 cm, márgenes enteros. Las flores atraen a los colibríes.
Hábitat: Orillas del arroyo, húmedos, arenosos, semí-sombreadas. Elevación 1656 m.
Distribución: Kansas, Carolina de Sur, Arizona, Nuevo México, Texas, México.
Comentarios: Fotografiada en septiembre a lo largo del Arroyo de EL Cajón en Tascate, Cerocahui.

Cinquefoil, Yerba Colorada
Potentilla thurberi

• Rose family Rosaceae
Plant: 17" tall.
Flower: 3/4" wide.
Description: Deep red radially symmetrical flower, small bowl shaped with scallops 3/4" x 3/4", darker towards the base, 5 pointed star pattern in center. Leaves alternate, 1–2" long, palmate-compound, fingerlike leaflets, margins toothed. Hairy stem.
Habitat: Dry stream bed, moist shade, sand. Elevation 5422'.
Range: Southwest, Rocky Mountains, Mexico.
Comments: Photographed in August near Paraiso del Oso above the Arroyo del Ranchito, Cerocahui.

• Familia de la rosa Rosaceae
Planta: de 43 cm de alto.
Flor: de 1.9 cm de ancho.
Descripción: Flor de color rojo oscuro, radialmente simétrica, formando una pequeña copa de 1.9 cm x 1.9 cm, más oscura en la base, mostrando una forma estrella de 5 puntos en el centro. Hojas alternas, palmeadamente compuestas de 2.5 a 5 cm de largo, con segmentos en forma de dedos, márgenes dentados. Tallos velludos.
Hábitat: Orillas de arroyo, húmedos, sombreados y arenosos. Elevación 1653 m.
Distribución: Suroeste, las Montañas Rocallosas, México.
Comentarios: Fotografiada en agosto cerca de Paraiso del Oso, arriba de Arroyo del Ranchito, Cerocahui.

Scarlet Creeper, Transpecos Morning Glory/
Ipomoea cristulata

Cinquefoil, Yerba Colorada/*Potentilla thurberi*

Red Radially Symmetrical

Columbine
Aquilegia skinneri
- Buttercup family Ranunculaceae

Plant: 30–45" tall.

Flower: 2 1/2–3" long, 3/4" wide.

Description: Red and green radially symmetrical nodding, scoop-shaped flower, 5 petals extending into backward projecting spur with many yellow stamens protruding from center of flower. Compound divided leaves 1 1/2–2" long, alternating, margins entire.

Habitat: Roadside, rocky cliff, moist, rock crevices, sun. Elevation 7381'.

Range: New Mexico and Chihuahua, Mexico.

Comments: Photographed in September on the road to Cerro Gallegos near Mesa de Arturo.

- Familia Ranunculaceae

Planta: de 76 a 114 cm de alto.

Flor: de 6.3 a 7.5 cm de largo, 1.9 cm de ancho.

Descripción: Flor roja a verde radialmente simétrica, colgante, 5 pétalos con una extensión en forma de espuela, con muchos estambres saliendo del centro de la flor; hojas palmeadamente compuestas, de 3.8–5 cm de largo, alternas, márgenes lisos.

Hábitat: Orillas de caminos, acantilados rocosos, grietas rocosas, húmedas, asoleado. Elevación 2250 m.

Distribución: Nuevo México y Chihuahua, México.

Comentarios: Fotografiada en septiembre sobre orilla de camino a Cerro Gallegos cerca del la Mesa de Arturo.

Red Daisy- and Dandelion-like

Zinnia, La India
Zinnia peruviana
- Aster family Asteraceae

Plant: 18–24" tall.

Flower: 1 1/2" wide.

Description: Small red daisy-like flower, 12 ray flowers on top of single stem plant. Leaves opposite, 2" long, lanceolate, margins entire. Visited by hummingbirds and butterflies.

Habitat: Rocky slope, sand, moist, semi-shade. Elevation 5462'.

Range: Southwestern U.S., Mexico, Central and South America.

Comments: Photographed in August behind Paraiso del Oso on a rocky slope near Arroyo del Ranchito, Cerocahui.

- Familia del girasol Asteraceae

Planta: de 45 a 60 cm de alto.

Cabezuela: de 3.8 cm de ancho.

Descripción: Pequeñas flores rojas dispuestas en una Cabezuela sostenida por brácteas, 12 flores liguladas, en la parte terminal de cada tallo. Hojas opuestas, 5 cm de largo, lanceoladas, márgenes enteros. Flores son visitadas por colibríes y mariposas.

Hábitat: Faldas rocosas, arenosos, húmedos y semi-sombreadas. Elevación 1665 m.

Distribución: Suroeste de USA, México, Centro y Sur América.

Comentarios: Fotografiada en agosto atras de Paraiso del Oso sobre una falda rocosa cerca de Arroyo del Ranchito, Cerocahui.

Columbine/*Aquilegia skinneri*

Zinnia, La India/*Zinnia peruviana*

Red Bilaterally Symmetrical

Maycoba Sage
Salvia betulifolia

• Mint family Lamiaceae
Plant: Shrub 4–6' tall.
Flower: 2–2 1/2" long, 1/2–1" wide.
Description: Red shrub, flower bilaterally symmetrical, tubular 2 lipped, upper lip lined in white with hairs, lower lip white stripe leading to throat, 3/4" sepals tinged with red. Flowers when opened look like the mouth of a snake. Woody stem. Leaves opposite, ovate, 1 1/2–1 3/4" long. Margins toothed.
Habitat: Lightly wooded area, rim of canyon, rocky and leaf compost, moist, semi-shade. Elevation 7900'.
Range: Durango and Chihuahua, Mexico.
Comments: Photographed in September at Sinforosa Canyon Park, 10.6 miles from Guachochi.

• Familia de la menta Lamiaceae
Planta: de 1.2 a 1.8 m de alto.
Flor: de 5–6.3 cm de largo, por 1.3–2.5 cm de ancho.
Descripción: Arbusto con flores bilateralmente simétricas, rojas, tubulares con 2 labios, el labio superior con vellosidades blancas, el labio inferior con rallas blancas conduciendo a la garganta del tubo, sépalos de 1.9 cm de largo manchados de rojo. Abierta, la flor se parece a la boca de una serpiente. Tallos leñosos. Hojas opuestas, ovadas, de 3.8 a 4.4 cm de largo, márgenes dentados.
Hábitat: Lugares arbustivos, borde del cañón, rocoso con mantillo presente, húmedo, semí-sombreado. Elevación 2708 m.
Distribución: Durango y Chihuahua, México.
Comentarios: Fotografiada en septiembre en el Parque del Cañón de la Sinforosa, 17 km de Guachochi.

Perennial Wild Poinsettia, Contrayerba
Euphorbia colorata

• Spurge family Euphorbiaceae
Plant: 6" tall.
Flower: 6" wide.
Description: Plant has 1 center stalk that branches into 3, 1 deep red bilaterally symmetrical flower per stem. Flower has 2 long bracts that go from red to green, 4 medium ones, and 4 smaller ones. Two apple-like balls in center of each flower. Alternate, linear leaves, 3–5" long, margins entire. Blooms in spring and fall.
Habitat: Rocky slope with loose rocks, loam, dry, sun. Elevation 7235'.
Range: Chihuahua, Durango, Sinaloa, Sonora, Zacatecas in Mexico.
Comments: Photographed in August at Rancho Sohauachi on the road from La Mesa de Arturo to Cerro Gallegos.

• Familia de la Candelilla Euphorbiaceae
Planta: de 15 cm de alto.
Flor: de 15 cm de ancho.
Descripción: La planta tiene un tallo principal el cual se ramifica en 3, con una flor roja bilateralmente simétrica sobre cada una. La flor tiene 2 brácteas largas que van desde rojas a verdes, 4 medianas y 4 mas pequeñas. Dos bolas en forma de manzana en el centro de cada flor. Hojas alternas, lineares, de 7.5 a 12.5 cm de largo, márgenes enteros. Florece en la primavera y otoño.
Hábitat: Faldas rocosas con rocas sueltas, franco, secas, asoleados. Elevación 2205 m.
Distribución: Chihuahua, Durango, Sinaloa, Sonora, Zacatecas en México.
Comentarios: Fotografiada en agosto en el Rancho Sohauachi, camino a la Mesa de Arturo.

Maycoba Sage/*Salvia betulifolia*

Perennial Wild Poinsettia, Contrayerba/
Euphorbia colorata

Red Elongated Clusters

Running Rusellia
Russelia sarmentosa

- Figwort family Scrophulariaceae

Plant: 22–26" tall.

Flower: 5/8–3/4" long, 1/8" wide.

Description: Red elongated cluster of bilaterally symmetrical tubular lipped flowers. Grows in long open cluster. Square woody stem. Ovate leaves, up to 3" long.

Habitat: Side of rocks, leaf debris, damp, sun. Elevation 7021'.

Range: Central America, Cuba, Mexico.

Comments: Photographed in September on the road to Cerro Gallegos near fountain.

- Familia Scrophulariaceae

Planta: de 56 a 66 cm de alto.

Flor: de 1.6 a 1.9 cm de largo, por 3 mm de ancho.

Descripción: Flores rojas, bilateralmente simétricas, tubulares. Las plantas crecen en grupo. Tallo leñoso, cuadrado. Hojas ovadas, hasta 7.5 cm de largo.

Hábitat: Junto a las rocas, sobre mantillo, húmedo, asoleado. Elevación 2140 m.

Distribución: América central, Cuba, México.

Comentarios: Fotografiada en septiembre sobre camino a Cerro Gallegos, cerca la fuente.

Scarlet Sage, Poleo del Campo
Stachys coccinea

- Mint family Lamiaceae

Plant: 12–36" tall.

Flower: 3/4" long.

Description: Scarlet-red elongated cluster, bilaterally symmetrical tubular 2 lipped flowers 1/2" x 3/4", single-lobed upper lip, tri-lobed lower lip in whorls. Leaves opposite, 2" long, lanceolate, margins toothed. Square stem.

Habitat: Near stream bed, rocky, moist, semi-shade. Elevation 5462'.

Range: Colorado, southern half of Southwest, Texas, northern Mexico.

Comments: Photographed in August behind Paraiso del Oso along Arroyo del Ranchito, near Cerocahui.

- Familia de la menta Lamiaceae

Planta: de 30 a 91 cm de alto.

Flor: de 1.9 cm de largo.

Descripción: Flores sobre inflorescencia alargadas, de color rojo escarlata, tubulares con dos labios, bilateralmente simétricas, de 1.3 cm x 1.9 cm, labio superior solitario, labio inferior tri-lobulado. Hojas opuestas, de 5 cm de largo, lanceoladas, márgenes dentados. Tallos cuadrados.

Hábitat: Orillas de arroyos, rocosas, húmedos, semi-sombreadas. Elevación 1665 m.

Distribución: Colorado, mitad sur del Suroeste, Texas, norte de México.

Comentarios: Fotografiada en agosto atras de Paraiso del Oso, a lo largo del Arroyo del Rancho, cerca de Cerocahui.

Running Rusellia/*Russelia sarmentosa*

Scarlet Sage, Poleo Del Campo/*Stachys coccinea*

Red Elongated Clusters

Penstemon apateticus

- Figwort family Scrophulariaceae
Plant: 16–20" tall.
Flower: 1 1/4–1 1/2" long, 1/2–5/8" wide.
Description: Red elongated cluster of bilaterally symmetrical tubular flowers, 2 lobed upper lip, 3 lobed lower lip, calyx holding each tube. Grows in long open cluster, stem rigid. Sparsely narrow linear leaves, progress from 1/2–3" down the stem. At base both linear and ovate leaves, margins entire.
Habitat: Rocky ground, shallow layer of soil, semi-moist, sun. Elevation 7783'.
Range: Michoacán, Durango, Chihuahua, Oaxaca, Guanajuato, Jalisco, Nayarit, Puebla, Sinaloa, Veracruz, Zacatecas in Mexico.
Comments: Photographed in September on the road to Cerro Gallegos, upper lookout, 5/6 of way to the top.

- Familia Scrophulariaceae
Planta: de 41 a 50 cm de alto.
Flor: de 3.1 a 3.8 cm de largo, por 1.3 a 1.6 cm de ancho.
Descripción: Flores sobre inflorescencia alargadas, tubulares, bilateralmente simétricas, 2 labios superiores y 3 labios inferiores, cáliz sosteniendo cada flor. Las plantas crecen en grupos, tallos rígidos. Hojas lineares, angostas, enchansándose hacia la base. En la base de la planta se encuentran ambas hojas lineares y ovadas, márgenes enteros.
Hábitat: Suelos rocosos, someros, semi-húmedos, asoleados. Elevación 2372 m.
Distribución: Michoacán, Nayarit, Durango, Chihuahua, Oaxaca, Guanajuato, Jalisco, Puebla, Sinaloa, Veracruz, Zacatecas en México.
Comentarios: Fotografiada en septiembre sobre camino al Cerro Gallegos, 5/6 parte del camino de la cima.

Penstemon roseus

- Figwort family Scrophulariaceae
Plant: 10–16" tall.
Flower: 1" long, 5/8–3/4" wide.
Description: Maroon elongated cluster, bilaterally symmetrical, 2-lipped tubular flowers, upper lip—2 lobed, lower lip—3 lobed, in whorls. Leaves opposite, linear, 3/4–1 1/2" long. Margins toothed.
Habitat: Roadside, rock and sand, dry, semi-shade. Elevation 6574'.
Range: Chihuahua, Durango, Guanajuato, Guerrero, Jalisco, Michoacán, San Luis Potosi, Sinaloa, Veracruz in Mexico.
Comments: Photographed in September on the road from Guachochi to Tónachi, 5.5 miles to left hand turn to Tónachi, then 12.4 miles.

- Familia Scrophulariaceae
Planta: de 25.4 a 41 cm de alto.
Flor: de 2.5 cm de largo, por 1.6 a 1.9 cm de ancho.
Descripción: Flores moradas, agrupadas en inflorescencia alargadas, bilateralmente simétricas, tubulares, labio superior con 2 lobulos, labio inferior con 3 lobulos. Hojas opuestas, lineares, de 1.9 a 3.8 cm de largo, márgenes dentados.
Hábitat: Orillas de camino, rocosas y arenosos, secas, semi-sombreadas. Elevación 2004 m.
Distribución: Chihuahua, Durango, Guanajuato, Guerrero, Jalisco, Michoacán, San Luis Potosí, Sinaloa, Veracruz en México.
Comentarios: Fotografiada en septiembre, camino de Guachochi a Tónachi, 8.9 km antes de dar vuelta a Tónachi, después 20 km.

Penstemon apateticus

Penstemon roseus

87

Red Elongated Clusters

Bat-Faced Monkey Flower, Yakén
Cuphea llavea

- Loosestrife family Lythraceae
Plant: 14–24" tall.
Flower: 1 1/4" long.
Description: Hairy red elongated cluster of bilaterally symmetrical tubular flowers 3/4" wide, 1 1/4" long, fuzzy violet ball and stamens sticking out under the end, two brilliant red petals (like ears), black veins lining each petal. Arrangement on stem one-side racemes. Leaves opposite, lanceolate, 3/4–1 1/2", margins entire.
Habitat: On moist rock cliff, sun. Elevation 4819'.
Range: Northern and central Mexico.
Comments: Photographed in August on the road coming out of the canyon from Urique.

- Familia Lythraceae
Planta: de 35.5 a 60 cm de alto.
Flor: de 3.1 cm de largo.
Descripción: Flores rojas, cubiertas de vellosidades sobre una inflorescencia alargada, bilateralmente simétricas, tubulares, estigma globosa de color violáceo y estambres saliendo del tubo; dos pétalos rojo vivo (parecidos a orejas); nervaduras negras sobre cada pétalo. Inflorescencia un racimo unilateral. Hojas opuestas, lanceoladas, de 1.9 a 3.8 cm de largo, márgenes enteros.
Hábitat: Sobre pendiente rocosa, humeda, asoleado. Elevación 1469 m.
Distribución: Norte y centro de México.
Comentarios: Fotografiada en agosto, camino saliendo del cañón de Urique.

Not Yet Identified

Plant: about 3' tall.
Description: Red succulent plant with red fleshy stem. Elongated cluster of long fleshy bilaterally symmetrical red tubular flowers facing upward. Stamens protrude out of flower on red stems with yellow tips. Flowers are along upper part of stem and bloom from bottom up. Stiff, pointed leaves at base with long hairs or prickles on margins. Tall flower stalk from base of leaves is similar to a yucca-type plant.
Habitat: Volcanic rock, leaf debris, dry, sun. Elevation 5710'.
Range: Chihuahua, Mexico.
Comments: Sighted and photographed in the spring by Bonnie Dirk at Mirador (highest point) on Tortuga Trail near Paraiso del Oso, Cerocahui.

Planta: de casi 90 cm de alto.
Descripción: Una planta roja suculenta con tallo carnoso y rojo. Flores rojas, carnosas, tubulares, sobre inflorescencia alargada, bilateralmente simétricas, orientadas hacia arriba. Estambres salientes con filamentos rojas y anteras amarillas. Flores terminales con floración desde la base del pedúnculo. Hojas rígidas, puntiagudas, básales, algo espinosas en los márgenes. Tallo floral parecido al escapo de la palmilla.
Hábitat: Sobre roca volcánica, con mantillo, seco, asoleado. Elevación 1740 m.
Distribución: Chihuahua, México.
Comentarios: Fotografiada en la primavera por Bonnie Dirk en el Mirador del camino Tortuga, cerca de Paraiso del Oso, Cerocahui.

Bat-Faced Monkey Flower, Yakén/*Cuphea llavea*

Not Yet Identified

Red Rounded Clusters

Firecracker Bush, Cigarrito
Bouvardia ternifolia

• Madder family Rubiaceae
Plant: 26" tall.
Flower: 1" long.
Description: Scarlet-red rounded loose clusters of radially symmetrical tubular flowers 1/4" x 1", 4 rounded point-tipped lobes at tip of leafy branches. Small shrub with numerous erect branches. Leaves opposite, 3–3 1/2" long, lanceolate, margins entire.
Habitat: Rocky slope, loam, dry, sun. Elevation 7235'.
Range: Texas, New Mexico, Arizona, northern Mexico.
Comments: Photographed in August at Rancho Sohauachi on the road from La Mesa de Arturo to Cerro Gallegos.

• Familia Rubiaceae
Planta: de 66 cm de alto.
Flor: de 2.5 cm de largo.
Descripción: Flores rojo escarlatas sobre inflorescencia abierta, tubulares, radialmente simétricas, de 6 mm x 2.5 cm, el tubo terminando en 4 lobulos puntiagudos. Pequeño arbusto con numerosos tallos, erectos. Hojas opuestas, de 7.5 a 8.8 cm de largo, lanceoladas, márgenes enteros.
Hábitat: Pendiente rocosa, suelo franco, seca, asoleada. Elevación 2205 m.
Distribución: Texas, Nuevo México, Arizona, norte de México.
Comentarios: Fotografiada en agosto en el Rancho Sohauachi, camino de la Mesa de Arturo al Cerro Gallegos.

Not Yet Identified

Plant: approximately 2–3' tall.
Description: Red and yellow rounded loose cluster of bilaterally symmetrical long red tubular flowers that flare to reveal a yellow throat. Leaves lanceolate in shape. The structure of the plant looks similar to the Mexican lobelia (*Lobelia laxiflora*), however, this identification has not been verified.
Habitat: Moist. Elevation 5610'.
Range: Chihuahua, Mexico.
Comments: Sighted and photographed in the spring by Bonnie Dirk off the Tascate–El Cajón trail before the box canyon, between Paraiso del Oso and Cerocahui.

Planta: de 60 a 90 cm de alto.
Descripción: Inflorescencia abierta de color rojo y amarillo, con flores rojas, tubulares, bilateralmente simétricas, con garganta amarilla. Hojas lanceoladas. Planta parecida a *Lobelia laxiflora*.
Hábitat: Suelos húmedo. Elevación 1710 m.
Distribución: Chihuahua, México.
Comentarios: Fotografiada en la primavera por Bonnie Dirk, sobre camino de Táscate a el Cajón, antes del cañón de caja, entre Paraiso del Oso y Cerocahui.

Firecracker Bush, Cigarrito/*Bouvardia ternifolia*

Not Yet Identified

Part Five Pink Flowers

Pink Radially Symmetrical

Gomphrena decumbens

• Amaranth family Amaranthaceae
Plant: 11" tall.
Flower: 3/8" wide.
Description: Red violet radial cluster (like clover), pointed petals, cradled by two small leaves. Rough stem. Opposite, lanceolate, rough leaves 1/2–1" long, margins entire.
Habitat: Up from stream bed, sand and rocks, moist, sun. Elevation 5471'.
Range: Bolivia, Guatemala, Paraguay, Mexico.
Comments: Photographed in September at Tascate between Paraiso del Oso and Cerocahui.

• Familia del quelite Amaranthaceae
Planta: de 28 cm de alto.
Flor: de 9 mm de ancho.
Descripción: Flores sobre una inflorescencia compacta de color rojo violáceo, radial, pétalos puntiagudos, sostenidos por dos brácteas pequeñas. Tallo rugoso. Hojas opuestas, lanceoladas, rugosas, de 1.3 a 2.5 cm de largo, márgenes enteros.
Hábitat: Orillas de arroyo, rocosas y arenosos, húmedas, asoleados. Elevación 1668 m.
Distribución: Bolivia, Guatemala, Paraguay, México.
Comentarios: Fotografiada en septiembre en Táscate entre Paraiso del Oso y Cerocahui.

Mountain Four O'clock
Mirabilis oblongifolia

• Four o'clock family Nyctaginaceae
Plant: 16" tall.
Flower: 1/2" wide.
Description: Dark pink radially symmetrical flower, 5 united petals, pink and white, pink stamens with yellow tips extend above flower. Leaves opposite, heart shaped, 1–2" long, velvety, hairs underside. Margins entire.
Habitat: Along road, rocky cliff, sand and rock, arid, sun. Elevation 4500'.
Range: Colorado, Arizona, Mexico.
Comments: Photographed in September on the road to San Ignacio, 5 miles from Batopilas.

• Familia de la bugambilia Nyctaginaceae
Planta: de 41 cm de alto.
Flor: de 1.3 cm de ancho.
Descripción: Planta con flores radialmente simétricas, de color rosa oscuro, 5 pétalos unidos, rosas y blancos, estambres rosados con anteras amarillas sobresalientes. Hojas opuestas, en forma de corazón, de 2.5 a 5 cm de largo, sedosas, velludas en el envés, márgenes enteros.
Hábitat: A lo largo del camino, pendiente rocosa, arenosa, seca, asoleado. Elevación 1372 m.
Distribución: Colorado, Arizona, México.
Comentarios: Fotografiada en septiembre en camino a San Ignacio, 8 km de Batopilas.

Gomphrena decumbens

Mountain Four O'clock/*Mirabilis oblongifolia*

Pink Radially Symmetrical

Spurred Anoda
Anoda cristata

• Mallow family Malvaceae
Plant: 12–18" tall.
Flower: 3/4" wide.
Description: Lavender radially symmetrical 5 petaled flower, striations on each petal, lobes on the end, white disk. Alternate, lobed leaves 3/4–1 1/2" long, margins entire.
Habitat: Ditch next to road, rocky, damp, sun. Elevation 7021'.
Range: Northeast, south, central, southwest U.S., Mexico.
Comments: Photographed in September on the road to Cerro Gallegos near La Cueva (basket cave).

• Familia del algodón Malvaceae
Planta: de 30 a 45 cm de alto.
Flor: de 1.9 cm de ancho.
Descripción: Flor lavanda, radialmente simétrica con 5 pétalos, estriadas, lobulados, con centro blanco. Hojas alternas, lobuladas, de 1.9 a 3.8 cm de largo, márgenes enteros.
Hábitat: Zanja cerca del camino, suelo rocoso, húmedo, asoleado. Elevación 2140 m.
Distribución: Noreste, sur, centro, suroeste de USA, México.
Comentarios: Fotografiada en septiembre en camino al Cerro Gallegos cerca de la Cueva.

Mexican Evening Primrose
Oenothera rosea

• Primrose family Onagraceae
Plant: 2–12" tall.
Flower: 5/8–1" wide.
Description: Pink flat radially symmetrical flower, white and green center, 4 petals, prominent stamens and pistil. Woody stem. Sprawls. Alternate, lanceolate leaves (some lobed near stem) 3/4–2" long, margins entire. Blooms in spring and fall.
Habitat: Along stream bed and opening in wooded forest, rocky, damp with water, sun. Elevation 5433' to 5610'.
Range: California, Arizona, Texas, Mexico, Costa Rica, Guatemala, Bolivia, Ecuador, Peru.
Comments: Photographed in September below Tortuga high vista, near Paraiso del Oso, Cerocahui.

• Familia Onagraceae
Planta: de 5 a 30 cm de alto.
Flor: 1.6 a 2.5 cm de ancho.
Descripción: Flor rosada, aplanada, radialmente simétrica, centro blanco y verde, 4 pétalos, estambres y pistilo prominentes. Tallo leñoso. Rastrera. Hojas alternas, lanceoladas (algunas lobuladas), de 1.9 a 5 cm de largo, márgenes enteros. Florece en primavera y otoño.
Hábitat: A lo largo del arroyo y aclareos del bosque, suelo rocoso, húmedo con agua, asoleado. Elevación 1656 a 1710 m.
Distribución: California, Arizona, Texas, México, Costa Rica, Guatemala, Bolivia, Ecuador, Perú.
Comentarios: Fotografiada en septiembre abajo de la Vista Alta de Tortuga, cerca del Paraiso del Oso, Cerocahui.

Spurred Anoda/*Anoda Cristata*

Mexican Evening Primrose/*Oenothera rosea*

Pink Radially Symmetrical

Crestrib Morning Glory
Ipomoea costellata
• Morning glory family Convolvulaceae
Plant: Vine.
Flower: 1 1/4" long, 1" wide.
Description: Fuchsia funnel shaped radially symmetrical flowers on vine. Palmately compound leaves 1/2–2" long, 5–9 segments, look like bird's feet, along one side of stem, margins entire.
Habitat: Under pine trees near stream, sandy loam, dry, semi-shade. Elevation 5455'.
Range: Texas, New Mexico, Arizona, Mexico, Guatemala.
Comments: Photographed in September on the trail to Cave of Crosses near stream and Paraiso del Oso, Cerocahui.

• Familia de la jicama Convolvulaceae
Planta: Trepadora.
Flor: de 3.1 cm de largo, por 2.5 de ancho.
Descripción: Flores en forma de embudo, radialmente simétricas, de color rosa. Hojas palmeadamente compuestas, de 1.3 a 5 cm de largo, con 5–9 segmentos, parecidos a la pata de un pato, saliendo sólo por un lado del tallo, márgenes enteros.
Hábitat: Abajo de los pinos, cerca de arroyo, suelo franco, seco, semí-húmedo. Elevación 1663 m.
Distribución: Texas, Nuevo México, Arizona, México, Guatemala.
Comentarios: Fotografiada en septiembre sobre camino a la Cueva de las Cruces, cerca de arroyo y del Paraiso del Oso, Cerocahui.

Common Four O'clock
Mirabilis jalapa
• Four o'clock family Nyctaginaceae
Plant: 34" tall.
Flower: 1 1/4" long, 1 1/4" wide.
Description: Magenta radially symmetrical, trumpet-shaped, 5 petal lobe flair flower, frequently seen in magenta, yellow, or white. Leaves opposite, 2" long, lanceolate, margins entire.
Habitat: Roadside next to houses, rocky soil, dry, sun. Elevation 5336'.
Range: Originally from Mexico then escaped into the wild.
Comments: Photographed in August on the roadside between Paraiso del Oso and Cerocahui.

• Familia de la bugambilea Nyctaginaceae
Planta: de 86 cm de alto.
Flor: de 3.1 cm de largo, por 3.1 cm de ancho.
Descripción: Flor de color magenta, radialmente simétrica, en forma de trompeta, 5 petalos a menudo de color magenta, amarillo o blanco. Hojas opuestas, de 5 cm de largo, lanceoladas, márgenes enteros.
Hábitat: Orillas de camino, cerca de las casas, suelo rocoso, seco, asoleado. Elevación 1626 m.
Distribución: Originalmente nativa de México, luego se hizo silvestre.
Comentarios: Fotografiada en agosto, sobre orilla de camino entre Paraiso del Oso y Cerocahui.

Crestrib Morning Glory/*Ipomoea costellata*

Common Four O'clock/*Mirabilis jalapa*

Pink Radially Symmetrical

Morning Glory, Camotito
Ipomoea capillacea

• Morning glory family Convolvulaceae
Plant: 3 1/2" tall.
Flower: 1 1/2" wide.
Description: Magenta funnel-shaped flower, 1 1/2" x 1 1/2", starts off white and goes into fuchsia, radially symmetrical, very low to the ground. Branching stem, multiple 1/2" small soft needles up the stem.
Habitat: Between rocks on hillside, sand, moist, sun. Elevation 5651'.
Range: Arizona, Texas, New Mexico, Mexico, South America.
Comments: Photographed in August off the east side of the road between Cerocahui and Bahuichivo.

• Familia de la jicama Convolvulaceae
Planta: de 8.8 cm de alto.
Flor: de 3.8 cm de ancho.
Descripción: Flor magenta en forma de embudo, de 3.8 cm x 3.8 cm, radialmente simétrica. Planta prostrada con tallos delgados.
Hábitat: Sobre lomas, suelo arenoso, húmedo, asoleado. Elevación 1722 m.
Distribución: Arizona, Texas, Nuevo México, México, Sur América.
Comentarios: Fotografiada en agosto sobre orilla este del camino entre Cerocahui y Bahuichivo.

Geranium

• Geranium family Geraniaceae
Plant: 15" tall.
Flower: 1 3/4" wide.
Description: Fuchsia radially symmetrical flower, 5 petals, white stripes radiating from center, stamens and pistil protrude 1/2" above flower. Leaves opposite, palmately lobed, 1 1/4–2" long. Margins toothed.
Habitat: Field by roadside, fine rocks, loam, moist, sun. Elevation 7740'.
Range: Chihuahua, Mexico.
Comments: Photographed in September after the left hand turn past Lago de Arareko, 6.2 miles from Creel.

• Familia del geranium Geraniaceae
Planta: de 37.5 cm de alto.
Flor: de 4.4 cm de ancho.
Descripción: Flor radialmente simétrica, rosa, 5 pétalos con rayas blancas desde el centro, estambres y pistilo salientes, media pulgada fuera de la flor. Hojas opuestas, palmeadamente lobuladas, de 3.1 a 5 cm de largo, márgenes dentados.
Hábitat: Orillas de caminos, suelo rocoso, franco, húmedo, asoleado. Elevación 2359 m.
Distribución: Chihuahua, México.
Comentarios: Fotografiada en septiembre después de la vuelta a la izquierda pasando el Lago Arareko, 10 km de Creel.

Morning Glory, Camotito/*Ipomoea capillacea*

Geranium

Pink Radially Symmetrical

Cosmos
Cosmos linearifolius

- Aster family Asteraceae
Plant: 22–26" tall.
Flower: 1 1/2–1 3/4" wide.
Description: Pink radially symmetrical 8 ray flower, 1/2" wide disk with several small flowers with 5 petals. Opposite, linear leaves 2–4 1/2" long, margins entire.
Habitat: Wooded area high plateau, rocky, damp, semi-shade. Elevation 5710'.
Range: Chihuahua, Durango, Sinaloa, Nayarit, Jaliso, Michoacán in Mexico.
Comments: Photographed in September near the vista on Tortuga hike near Paraiso del Oso, Cerocahui.

- Familia del girasol Asteraceae
Planta: de 56 a 66 cm de alto.
Flor: 3.8 a 4.4 cm de ancho.
Descripción: Cabezuela compuesta de 8 flores liguladas, dispuestas radialmente, flores tubulares numerosas, con 5 pétalos. Hojas opuestas, lineares, de 5 a 11.5 cm de largo, márgenes enteros.
Hábitat: Area boscosa sobre meseta alta, suelo rocoso, húmedo, semi-sombreado. Elevación 1740 m.
Distribución: Chihuahua, Durango, Sinaloa, Nayant, Jalisco, Michoacán en México.
Comentarios: Fotografiada en septiembre cerca del mirador del camino de Tortuga, cerca de Paraiso del Oso, Cerocahui.

Mexican Aster
Cosmos bipinnatus

- Aster family Asteraceae
Plant: 23–38" tall.
Flower: 3/4–2" wide.
Description: Pink and pink fading to white radially symmetrical flower, 8 rays, yellow disk. Compound, threadlike leaves, opposite, 1 1/2–2 1/2" long.
Habitat: Volcanic meadow, rocky with some soil, dry, sun. Elevation 5432' to 5639'.
Range: Ontario and Quebec, Canada; Netherlands Antilles; southwestern U.S.; Mexico.
Comments: Photographed in September at El Ranchito up on a mountain behind Paraiso del Oso, Cerocahui.

- Familia del girasol Asteraceae
Planta: de 58 a 96.5 cm de alto.
Flor: de 1.9 a 5 cm de ancho.
Descripción: Cabezuela formada por 8 flores liguladas rosas, cambiando a blanco cuando secas, dispuestas en forma radial, flores tubulares amarillas. Hojas compuestas, opuestas, con segmentos lineares, de 3.8 a 6.3 cm de largo.
Hábitat: Llano volcánico, rocoso con algo de suelo, seco, asoleado. Elevación 1656 a 1719 m.
Distribución: Ontario y Quebec, Canada; Antillas; Suroeste de USA; México.
Comentarios: Fotografiada en septiembre en el Ranchito, arriba de la loma atras de Paraiso del Oso, Cerocahui.

Cosmos/*Cosmos linearifolius*

Mexican Aster/*Cosmos bipinnatus*

Pink Radially Symmetrical

Cosmos, Jube
Cosmos

• Aster family Asteraceae
Plant: 24" tall.
Flower: 1 1/4–2" wide.
Description: Pale orchid radially symmetrical flower, 8 broad, rounded ray flowers, yellow center. Leaves opposite, threadlike, twice-pinnate, 1 1/2–2" long. Most of leaves in a basal cluster.
Habitat: Between rocks on a hillside, sand, moist, sun. Elevation 5651'.
Range: Chihuahua, Mexico.
Comments: Photographed in August off the road on the east side between Cerocahui and Bahuichivo.

• Familia del girasol Asteraceae
Planta: de 60 cm de alto.
Flor: de 3.1 a 5 cm de ancho.
Descripción: Cabezuela con 8 flores liguladas redondas, grandes, radialmente dispuestas, de color rojo pálido, flores tubulares amarillas. Hojas opuestas, segmentadas con segmentos lineares, de 3.8 a 5 cm de largo. La mayoria de las hojas básales.
Hábitat: Sobre lomas rocosas, suelo arenoso, húmedo, asoleado. Elevación 1722 m.
Distribución: Chihuahua, México.
Comentarios: Fotografiada en agosto sobre orilla este del camino entre Cerocahui y Bahuichivo.

Fourwing Evening Primrose
Oenothera tetraptera

• Evening primrose family Onagraceae
Plant: 7" tall.
Flower: 2–3" wide.
Description: Pink radially symmetrical flower, 4 petals, white stripes radiating from center, calyx folding together to form a scoop, one blossom per stem. Toothed lanceolate leaves, 1–2 1/2" long, starts out opposite, then alternate, red center vein in basal rosette.
Habitat: Heavily wooded small river valley bluff, rocky sand, moist, shade. Elevation 5700'.
Range: Texas and Chihuahua, Mexico.
Comments: Photographed in September on the trail to Huicochi (waterfall), near Cerocahui.

• Familia Onagraceae
Planta: de 17.5 de alto.
Flor: de 5 a 7.5 cm de ancho.
Descripción: Flor morada radialmente simétrica, 4 pétalos, rayados de blanco desde el centro, cáliz plegado para forma una copa, una flor por tallo. Hojas dentadas, lanceoladas, 2.5–6.3 cm de largo, las básales opuestas y luego alternas, nerviación central roja en una roseta basal.
Hábitat: Lugares húmedos, rocoso-arenosos, sombreados a lo largo del río. Elevación 1737 m.
Distribución: Texas y Chihuahua, México.
Comentarios: Fotografiada en septiembre sobre camino a la cascada, cerca de Cerocahui.

Cosmos, Jube/*Cosmos*

Fourwing Evening Primrose/*Oenothera tetraptera*

103

Pink Daisy- and Dandelion-like

Perezia wislizeni

- Aster family Asteraceae

Plant: 18–24" tall.

Flower: 1 3/4" wide.

Description: Cerise dandelion-like flower, many ray flowers, 1 1/4" receptacle that resembles a basket. Leaves alternate, oblong, 1–6" long, very stiff and clasping. Margins finely toothed.

Habitat: Side of road, lightly wooded area, dark fertile soil, moist, sun/shade. Elevation 6574'.

Range: Durango, Chihuahua, Jalisco in Mexico.

Comments: Photographed in September on the road from Guachochi to Sinforosa Canyon, 6 miles from Guachochi.

- Familia del girasol Asteraceae

Planta: de 45 a 60 cm de alto.

Flor: de 4.4 cm de ancho.

Descripción: Cabezuela con muchas flores liguladas, color rojo pálido, receptáculo de 3.1 cm parecido a canasta. Hojas alternas, oblongas, de 2.5 a 15 cm de largo, muy rígidas, márgenes finamente dentados.

Hábitat: Orilla de camino, ligeramente boscosa, suelo oscuro fértil, húmedo, semí-asoleada. Elevación 2004 m.

Distribución: Durango, Chihuahua, Jalisco en México.

Comentarios: Fotografiada en septiembre, camino de Guachochi al Cañón de la Sinforosa, 9.7 km de Guachochi.

Basket Flower, American Star-thistle

Centaurea americana

- Aster family Asteraceae

Plant: 20" tall.

Flower: 4" wide.

Description: Large lavender daisy-like head, threadlike disk flowers on outer border, white disk flowers in center. Flower head held by 1/2" receptacle that looks like a woven basket. Leaves alternate, lanceolate, 2" long, margins entire.

Habitat: Hillside with loose rocks, dry, sun, sand. Elevation 5403'.

Range: Central and southwestern U.S. and Chihuahua, Mexico.

Comments: Photographed in September on the hillside above Arroyo de El Cajón near Cerocahui.

- Familia del girasol Asteraceae

Planta: de 50 cm de alto.

Flor: de 10 de ancho.

Descripción: Cabezuela grande con flores de color lavanda, flores tubulares con pétalos lineares en la periferia, y los centrales con pétalos blancos. La cabezuela esta sostenida por un receptáculo de media pulgada que se parece a una pequeña canasta tejida. Hojas alternas, lanceoladas, 5 cm de largo y márgenes lisos.

Hábitat: Falda de cerros con piedras y arenas, ambiente seco y asoleado. Elevación 1647 m.

Distribución: Centro y suroeste de U.S.A. y Chihuahua, México.

Comentarios: Fotografiada en septiembre en loma arriba del arroyo El Cajón cerca de Cerocahui.

Perezia wislizeni

Basket Flower, American Star-thistle/
Centaurea americana

Pink Daisy- and Dandelion-like

Iosotephane heterophylla

- Aster family Asteraceae

Plant: 48" tall.

Flower: 4 1/2" wide.

Description: Large daisy-like flower, orchid and white ray flowers, 12–14 petals, disk 1 1/4" across, rigid stem. Rough, lobed, and toothed basal leaves 10–12" long. The roots are popular in Mexican traditional medicine.

Habitat: Pine forest, side of access road, heavily wooded, leaf debris over rock, moist, semi-shade. Elevation 7276'.

Range: From Chihuahua to Oaxaca in Mexico.

Comments: Photographed in September on the road to Cerro Gallegos, high lookout, near ranchito.

- Familia del girasol Asteraceae

Planta: de 122 cm de alto.

Flor: de 11.5 cm de ancho.

Descripción: Cabezuela grande formada por 12 a 14 flores liguladas grandes, de color blanco y rosa, conjunto de flores tubulares con un diámetro de 3.1 cm. Tallo rígido. Hojas rugosas, lobuladas y dentadas, básales de 25.4 a 30 cm de largo. Las raíces son populares en la medicina tradicional mexicana.

Hábitat: Bosque de pino, orilla de camino, en área densamente boscosa, suelo cubierto de mantillo y hojarasca, húmedo, semí-sombreado. Elevación 2218 m.

Distribución: De Chihuahua a Oaxaca en México.

Comentarios: Fotografiada en septiembre, camino al Cerro Gallegos, en el mirador, cerca del Ranchito.

Pink Bilaterally Symmetrical

Chihuahua Vervain, Vervaina
Verbena pinetorum

- Verbena family Verbenaceae

Plant: 12–13" tall.

Flower: 1/4" wide.

Description: Orchid bilaterally symmetrical flowers 1/4" x 1/2", 5 petal-like lobes. Blooms around stem from bottom up. Several branches upper part of plant. Leaves opposite, 1 1/2" long, margins toothed.

Habitat: Rocky, dry, sun. Elevation 5442'.

Range: Arizona, northern and central Mexico.

Comments: Photographed in August on the left side of the road near Paraiso del Oso heading toward Bahuichivo.

- Familia del Oreganillo Verbenaceae

Planta: de 30 a 33 cm de alto.

Flor: de 6 mm de ancho.

Descripción: Flores bilateralmente simétricas, de color rosa pálido, de 6 mm x 1.3 cm, con 5 pétalos. Tallos ramificados con inflorescencias grandes, desde la base de los tallos. Hojas opuestas, de 3.8 cm de largo, márgenes dentados.

Hábitat: Area rocosa, seca, asoleado. Elevación 1659 m.

Distribución: Arizona, norte y centro de México.

Comentarios: Fotografiada en agosto sobre orilla este del camino cerca de Paraiso del Oso yendo hacia Bahuichivo.

Iosotephane heterophylla

Chihuahua Vervain, Vervaina/*Verbena pinetorum*

Pink Bilaterally Symmetrical

Purple Scalystem
Elytraria imbricate

• Acanthus family Acanthaceae
Plant: 2" tall.
Flower: 3/8" wide.
Description: Small lavender bilaterally symmetrical flower. Blooms at ends of thick stems that look braided. Plant grows low to ground between rock crevices. Fuzzy, basal, lanceolate leaves 1 1/4–2 1/4" long, margins entire.
Habitat: Between volcanic rock, scant soil, dry, sun. Elevation 5639'.
Range: Texas, Arizona, New Mexico, Mexico, South America.
Comments: Photographed in September near El Ranchito up on the mountain behind Paraiso del Oso, Cerocahui.

• Familia Acanthaceae
Planta: de 5 cm de alto.
Flor: de 9 mm de ancho.
Descripción: Planta con una pequeña flor lavanda, bilateralmente simétrica, al terminal de un tallo grueso. Planta con crecimiento prostrado, en espacios entre las rocas. Hojas básales, lanceoladas, velludas, de 3.1 a 5.7 cm de largo, márgenes enteros.
Hábitat: Entre rocas volcánicas, suelo seco, asoleado. Elevación 1719 m.
Distribución: Texas, Arizona, Nuevo México, Sur América.
Comentarios: Fotografiada en septiembre cerca de El Ranchito, arriba del cerro atras de Paraiso del Oso, Cerocahui.

Phaseolus

• Pea family Fabaceae
Plant: Vine.
Flower: 3/4" long, 1/2" wide.
Description: Pink bilaterally symmetrical flower, 3 petals on long raceme. Three leaflets, 1 1/4" long, lanceolate, margins entire. Both flowers and leaves on 8" stem that rises above creeping vine.
Habitat: Volcanic rock above stream, loam, moist, sun. Elevation 5462'.
Range: Chihuahua, Mexico.
Comments: Photographed in August behind Paraiso del Oso above Arroyo del Ranchita, near Cerocahui.

• Familia del frijol Fabaceae
Planta: Trepadora.
Flor: de 1.9 cm de largo, por 1.3 cm de ancho.
Descripción: Planta con una flor rosa bilateralmente simétrica, 3 pétalos sobre un racimo largo. Hojas trifoliadas, foliolos lanceolados, de 3.1 cm de largo, márgenes enteros. Flores y hojas dispuestas sobre el tallo floral de 20 cm de largo.
Hábitat: Rocas volcánicas arriba del arroyo, suelo franco, húmedo, asoleado. Elevación 1665 m.
Distribución: Chihuahua, México.
Comentarios: Fotografiada en agosto atras de Paraiso del Oso, arriba del Arroyo El Ranchito, cerca de Cerocahui.

Purple Scalystem/*Elytraria imbricate*

Phaseolus

Pink Bilaterally Symmetrical

Not Yet Identified
- Pea family Fabaceae

Plant: Vine.
Flower: 1 1/4" long, 1/2" wide.
Description: Mulberry tubular flower, bilaterally symmetrical, flair with 1 petal at top, 2 smaller ones at bottom. Underneath flower white with orchid on tip. Leaves compound, lanceolate, 1" long, margins entire. Vine grows around other plants.
Habitat: Volcanic rock, moist, semi-shade. Elevation 5406'.
Range: Chihuahua, Mexico.
Comments: Photographed in August on a steep rocky hillside above Arroyo del Tortuga near Paraiso del Oso, Cerocahui.

- Familia del frijol Fabaceae

Planta: Trepadora.
Flor: de 3.1 cm de largo, por 1.3 cm de ancho.
Descripción: Planta con una flor tubular de color morado, bilateralmente simétrica, 1 pétalo arriba y 2 más pequeños abajo. La flor es blanca en su cara inferior con punta rosa. Hojas compuesta, lanceolada, de 2.5 cm de largo, márgenes enteros. Una trepadora que crece cerca de otras plantas.
Hábitat: Roca volcánica, húmeda, semi-sombreada. Elevación 1648 m.
Distribución: Chihuahua, México.
Comentarios: Fotografiada en agosto sobre una pendiente profunda arriba del Arroyo del Tortuga cerca de Paraiso del Oso, Cerocahui.

Cologania obovata
- Pea family Fabaceae

Plant: Vine.
Flower: 3/4" long, 3/4" wide.
Description: Vine with bilaterally symmetrical fuchsia flowers, like a hood with two wings, fuchsia inside hood and top of wings, white outside hood and under wings. Trifoliate ovate leaves, 3/4" long, margins entire. Bulb.
Habitat: Hillside above stream, rocky sand, moist, semi-shade. Elevation 5436'.
Range: Arizona, Mexico.
Comments: Photographed in September on the hillside above Arroyo del Ranchito near Paraiso del Oso, Cerocahui.

- Familia del frijol Fabaceae

Planta: Trepadora.
Flor: de 1.9 cm de largo, por 1.9 cm de ancho.
Descripción: Una trepadora con flores bilateralmente simétricas de color rosa pálida, como un capuchón con dos alas, color rosa a dentro del capuchón y arriba de las alas, blanco afuera del capuchón y por debajo de las alas. Hojas trifoliadas, foliolos ovados, de 1.9 cm de largo, márgenes enteros. Bulbo presente.
Hábitat: Pendiente arriba del arroyo, rocosa, arenosa, húmeda, semí-sombreada. Elevación 1657 m.
Distribución: Arizona, México.
Comentarios: Fotografiada en septiembre sobre pendiente arriba del Arroyo del Ranchito cerca de Paraiso del Oso, Cerocahui.

Not Yet Identified

Cologania obovata

Pink Bilaterally Symmetrical

Agalinis peduncularis

- Figwort family Scrophulariaceae
Plant: 15" tall.
Flower: 1" long, 1" wide.
Description: Fuchsia bilaterally symmetrical flower, hairy throat, white with fuchsia dots, long narrow tongue, funnel that flairs into 5 joined petals. Leaves opposite and alternate, very narrow linear, 3/4–1" long. Margins entire.
Habitat: Off roadside, rocky loam, dry, sun. Elevation 7536'.
Range: Guatemala, Mexico.
Comments: Photographed in September on the way out of Choquita, 4.3 miles from Creel.

- Familia Scrophulariaceae
Planta: de 37.5 cm de alto.
Flor: de 2.5 cm de largo, por 2.5 cm de ancho.
Descripción: Planta con una flor rosa, bilateralmente simétrica, garganta velluda, con puntos rosas, formando un tubo largo como un embudo, terminando con 5 pétalos unidos. Hojas opuestas y alternas, muy angostas, de 1.9 a 2.5 cm de largo, márgenes enteros.
Hábitat: Orillas de camino, suelo franco, rocoso, seco, asoleado. Elevación 2297 m.
Distribución: Guatemala, México.
Comentarios: Fotografiada en septiembre saliendo de Choguita, 7 km de Creel.

Espuela del Diablo
Proboscidea fragrans

- Pedalium family Pedaliaceae
Plant: 18–24" tall.
Flower: 2" long, 1 1/4" wide.
Description: Mauve, red violet, and white bilaterally symmetrical flower, tubular with 5 lobes, 3 lower mauve, 2 upper red violet, throat white with yellow stripes, red violet dots. Plant has sticky hairs. Leaves opposite and alternate, heart-shaped, 1 3/4–6 1/2" long. Margins lobed. Flowers fragrant. Large, clawlike seed pods when dried.
Habitat: Side of creek bed, sand, wet, semi-shade. Elevation 1955'.
Range: From Texas to northern Mexico.
Comments: Photographed in September in Arroyo Los Tachos, Batopilas.

- Familia del garambullo Pedaliaceae
Planta: de 45 a 60 cm de alto.
Flor: de 5 cm de largo, por 3.1 cm de ancho.
Descripción: Planta con una flor bilateralmente simétrica, bicolor, rojo violácea y blanca, tubular con 5 lobulos, 3 labios color malva y 2 superiores rojo violáceos, garganta blanca con rayas amarillas y puntos violáceos. Pelos pegajosos sobre la planta. Hojas opuestas y alternas, en forma de corazón, de 4.4 a 16.3 cm de largo, flores aromáticas márgenes lobulados. Fruto una capsula con dos largos cuernos cuando secos.
Hábitat: Orillas de arroyo, arenosos, húmedas, semí-sombreadas. Elevación 596 m.
Distribución: de Texas al norte de México.
Comentarios: Fotografiada en septiembre en el Arroyo Los Tachos, Batopilas.

Agalinis peduncularis

Espuela del Diablo/*Proboscidea fragrans*

Pink Elongated Clusters
Agastache

- Mint family Lamiaceae
Plant: 18" tall.
Flower: 1/2" long, 1/8" wide.
Description: Orchid elongated cluster of bilaterally symmetrical tubular 2-lipped flowers. Calyx green to dark orchid, 1/2" long, 5 points. Leaves opposite, heart-shaped, 3/4–1" long. Margins toothed.
Habitat: Along side trail, sloped bank, rock, leaf compost, wet, shade. Elevation 5548'.
Range: Chihuahua, Mexico.
Comments: Photographed in September on a logging side road, canyon trail, Tascate, Cerocahui.

- Familia de la menta Lamiaceae
Planta: de 45 cm de alto.
Flor: de 1.3 cm de largo, por 3 mm de ancho.
Descripción: Flores sobre un racimo alargado, de color rosa, bilateralmente simétricas, con dos labios. Cáliz verde a rosa oscuro, de 1.3 cm de largo, con 5 puntos. Hojas opuestas, en forma de corazón, de 1.9 a 2.5 cm de largo, márgenes dentados.
Hábitat: A lo largo de la brecha, sobre pendiente, roca, hojarasca presente, húmeda, sombreada. Elevación 1691 m.
Distribución: Chihuahua, México.
Comentarios: Fotografiada en septiembre sobre camino de los troceros, camino en el cañón, Táscate, Cerocahui.

Pale Giant Hyssop
Agastache pallida

- Mint family Lamiaceae
Plant: 9–18" tall.
Flower: 1 1/4" long, 1/4" wide.
Description: Pink/violet elongated cluster of bilaterally symmetrical tubular flowers, 2 upper petals, 2 side petals, larger lower toothed petal. Pistil and stamens extend beyond the flower. Leaves opposite, cordate, 1/2–1 1/2" long. Margins toothed.
Habitat: Hillside between rocks, soil hard packed sand, dry, sun. Elevation 7672'.
Range: Arizona and Chihuahua, Durango, Sonora in Mexico.
Comments: Photographed in September after a left hand turn into San Ignacio, 5 miles from Creel.

- Familia de la menta Lamiaceae
Planta: de 22.5 a 45 cm de alto.
Flor: de 3.1 cm de largo, por 6 mm de ancho.
Descripción: Flores sobre un racimo alargado, bilateralmente simétricas, 2 labios superiores y 2 inferiores, los más grandes dentados. Pistilo y estambres salientes. Hojas opuestas, cordadas, de 1.3 a 3.8 cm de largo, márgenes dentados.
Hábitat: Pendientes, suelo compacto, arenoso, seco, asoleado. Elevación 2338 m.
Distribución: Arizona y Chihuahua, Durango, Sonora en México.
Comentarios: Fotografiada en septiembre despues de la vuelta a la izquierda a San Ignacio, 8 km de Creel.

Agastache

Pale Giant Hyssop/*Agastache pallida*

115

Pink Elongated Clusters

Lemmon's Sage
Salvia lemmonii

- Mint family Lamiaceae

Plant: 15–20" tall.

Flower: 3/4" long, 3/8" wide.

Description: Violet red elongated cluster, upward, angled bilaterally symmetrical 2 lipped tubular flower, lower lip—4 lobed, upper lip like a beak with 2 small protrusions—one down, one curled back. Calyx 1/4" long. Leaves opposite, lanceolate, 1/2–1" long. Margins toothed.

Habitat: Along trail to waterfall, sloped face leading to ravine, rocky, leaf compost, damp, shade/sun. Elevation 5480'.

Range: Arizona, New Mexico, and Sonora, Chihuahua in Mexico.

Comments: Photographed in September on the trail to Cascada Huicochi, one-third of the way from the trailhead, Cerocahui.

- Familia de la menta Lamiaceae

Planta: de 37.5 a 50 cm de alto.

Flor: de 1.9 cm de largo, por 9 mm de ancho.

Descripción: Flores tubulares bilateralmente simétricas, bilabiadas de color violáceo y rojo, sobre un racimo alargado, labio inferior con 4 lobulos, labio superior como un gancho con 2 lobulos. Cáliz de 6 mm de largo. Hojas opuestas, lanceoladas, de 1.3 a 2.5 cm de largo, márgenes dentados.

Hábitat: A lo largo del camino a la cascada, sobre pendiente, rocosa, con mantillo, húmeda, sombreada y asoleado. Elevación 1670 m.

Distribución: Arizona, Nuevo México y Sonora, Chihuahua en México.

Comentarios: Fotografiada en septiembre sobre camino a la Cascada Huicochi, tercera parte del principio del camino, Cerocahui.

Lamourouxia viscosa

- Figwort family Scrophulariaceae

Plant: 24–38" tall.

Flower: 1/2–2" long, 1/4–3/8" wide.

Description: Magenta elongated cluster of bilaterally symmetrical tubular flowers, 2 lipped, prominent pistil coming out upper lip, curled lower lip. Upper and lower lip lined with white hairs. Blooms from the bottom up. Also seen in red and deep red. Fleshy 1/4" round stem. Opposite, lanceolate, fuzzy toothed leaves, 1/2–3 1/2" long.

Habitat: Rock cliff at rim of canyon, arid, semi-shade or sun. Elevation 6528 to 7900'.

Range: Belize, Costa Rica, El Salvador, Guatemala, Honduras, Nicaragua, Panama, and Mexico.

Comments: Photographed in September at Cerro Gallegos lower lookout.

- Familia Scrophulariaceae

Planta: de 60 a 96.5 cm de alto.

Flor: de 1.3 a 5 cm de largo, por 6 a 9 mm de ancho.

Descripción: Flores sobre un racimo alargado, de color magenta, bilabiadas, pistilo prominente, labios con pelos blancos. Flores también de color rojo a rojo oscuro. Tallos carnosos. Hojas opuestas, lanceoladas, peludas, dentadas, de 1.3 a 8.8 cm de largo.

Hábitat: Pendiente sobre orilla del cañón, seca, semí-sombreada o asoleada. Elevación 1990 a 2408 m.

Distribución: Belice, Costa Rica, El Salvador, Guatemala, Honduras, Nicaragua, Panamá y México.

Comentarios: Fotografiada en septiembre en el Cerro Gallegos, mirador de abajo.

Lemmon's Sage/*Salvia lemmonii*

Lamourouxia viscosa

Pink Elongated Clusters

Tripogandra purpurascens

• Spiderwort family Commelinaceae
Plant: 12" tall.
Flower: 1/2" wide.
Description: Light orchid elongated cluster of bilaterally symmetrical 3 petaled flowers. Multiple hairs protrude out center of flower. Leaves clasping, 1 1/2–2" long, lanceolate, margins entire.
Habitat: Top of slope on volcanic rock, sand, moist, sun. Elevation 5521'.
Range: Central and South America, Mexico.
Comments: Photographed in August on the east side of the road between Paraiso del Oso and Bahuichivo, near Cerocahui.

• Familia Commelinaceae
Planta: de 30 cm de alto.
Flor: de 1.3 cm de ancho.
Descripción: Flores de color rosa pálido, bilateralmente simétricas, sobre un tallo alargado, con tres pétalos, y vellosidades saliendo del centro de la flor. Hojas envainadas, de 3.8 a 5 cm de largo, lanceoladas, márgenes enteros.
Hábitat: Sobre pendiente con rocas volcánicas, húmeda, arenosa, asoleado. Elevación 1683 m.
Distribución: América central y del sur, México.
Comentarios: Fotografiada en agosto en el lad oeste del camino entre Paraiso del Oso y Bahuichivo, cerca de Cerocahui.

Tripogandra amplexicaulis

• Spiderwort family Commelinaceae
Plant: 14–18" tall.
Flower: 3/4" wide.
Description: Pink elongated cluster of bilaterally symmetrical 3 petaled flowers, white and yellow stamens protruding from center. Leaves lanceolate, 1 1/4–2 1/2" long, clasping, margins entire.
Habitat: On volcanic rock growing in shallow leaf debris, moist, loam, sun. Elevation 5690'.
Range: Guatemala, Nicaragua, Mexico.
Comments: Photographed in September on a volcanic plateau in between Cave of Crosses and Cave of Skull, Cerocahui.

• Familia Commelinaceae
Planta: de 35.5 a 45 cm de alto.
Flor: de 1.9 cm de ancho.
Descripción: Flores de color rosa, bilateralmente simétricas, dispuestas sobre un tallo alargado, con 3 pétalos, estambres blancos y amarillos saliendo del centro. Hojas lanceoladas, de 3.8 a 5 cm de largo, envainadas, márgenes enteros.
Hábitat: Sobre roca volcánica creciendo sobre mantillo, húmedo, franco, asoleado. Elevación 1734 m.
Distribución: Guatemala, Nicaragua, México.
Comentarios: Fotografiada en septiembre sobre una meseta volcanica entre la cueva de las Cruces y la Cueva del craneo, Cerocahui.

Tripogandra purpurascens

Tripogandra amplexicaulis

119

Pink Elongated Clusters

Santa Rita Mountain Ticktrefoil

Desmodium retinens

- Pea family Fabaceae

Plant: Vine 10–24" long.

Flower: 1/2–3/4" wide.

Description: Vine, fuchsia elongated cluster of bilaterally symmetrical flowers. Trifoliate compound leaves 1 1/2–1 3/4" long, margins entire.

Habitat: Volcanic plateau, rocky, some soil, dry, sun. Elevation 5639'.

Range: Arizona, Guatemala, Mexico.

Comments: Photographed in September near El Ranchito up on a mountain behind Paraiso del Oso, Cerocahui.

- Familia del frijol Fabaceae

Planta: Rastrera de 25.4 a 60 cm de largo.

Flor: de 1.3 a 1.9 cm de ancho.

Descripción: Una Rastrera, con flores bilateralmente simétricas, de color rosa. Hojas compuestas, trifoliadas, de 3.8 a 4.4 cm de largo, márgenes de los foliolos enteros.

Hábitat: Sobre meseta volcánica, rocosa, suelo someros, seco, asoleado. Elevación 1719 m.

Distribución: Arizona, Guatemala, México.

Comentarios: Fotografiada en septiembre cerca de El Ranchito arriba del cero atras de Paraiso del Oso, Cerocahui.

Desmodium madrense

- Pea family Fabaceae

Plant: 36–54" tall.

Flower: 1/2–3/4" wide.

Description: Small pea-like orchid bilaterally symmetrical flowers, elongated clusters. Stems are bending branches with short hairs. Compound palmate opposite leaves, 1–3 1/2" long, margins entire, rough outer surface.

Habitat: Wooded river valley, side of trail, rocky sand, moist, shade. Elevation 5609'.

Range: Chihuahua, Jalisco, and Nayarit in Mexico.

Comments: Photographed in September on the trail to Huicochi (waterfall) near Cerocahui.

- Familia del frijol Fabaceae

Planta: de 91 a 137 cm de alto.

Flor: de 1.3 a 1.9 cm de ancho.

Descripción: Pequeñas flores sobre un racimo alargado, de color rosa, bilateralmente simétricas. Tallos cubiertos de vellosidades cortas. Hojas compuestas, palmeadas, opuestas, de 2.5 a 8.8 cm de largo, márgenes enteros, con el haz rugoso.

Hábitat: Valle del río con árboles, sobre orilla de una brecha, rocosa, arenosa, húmeda, sombreada. Elevación 1710 m.

Distribución: Chihuahua, Jalisco y Nayarit en México.

Comentarios: Fotografiada en septiembre sobre camino a la cascada de Huicochi cerca de Cerocahui.

Santa Rita Mountain Ticktrefoil/*Desmodium retinens*

Desmodium madrense

Pink Elongated Clusters

Salt Spring Checkerbloom
Sidalcea neomexicana

• Mallow family Malvaceae
Plant: 8 1/2" tall.
Flower: 1" long, 1" wide.
Description: Violet/pink elongated cluster of radially symmetrical flowers, 5 striated and notched petals. Mostly basal leaves, one on stem, palmately lobed 3/4–1 1/2" long.
Habitat: Open field, hard packed sandy loam, dry, sun. Elevation 7641'.
Range: Arizona, California, Colorado, Idaho, New Mexico, Nevada, Oregon, Utah, Wyoming, Mexico.
Comments: Photographed in September after a left hand turn into San Ignacio, 4.5 miles from Creel.

• Familia del algodón Malvaceae
Planta: de 21.3 cm de alto.
Flor: de 2.5 cm de largo, por 2.5 cm de ancho.
Descripción: Flores violáceas/rosas, sobre un racimo alargado, radialmente simétricas, 5 pétalos estriadas y hendidos. Hojas en su mayoria básales, una sobre el tallo, palmeadamente lobuladas, de 1.9 a 3.8 cm de largo.
Hábitat: Llano abierto, suelo compacto, arenosos, franco, seco, asoleado. Elevación 2329 m.
Distribución: Arizona, California, Colorado, Idaho, Nuevo Mexico, Nevada, Oregon, Utah, Wyoming, México.
Comentarios: Fotografiada en septiembre despues de la vuelta a la izquierda a San Ignacio, 7.7 km de Creel.

Begonia, Agritos
Begonia gracilis

• Begonia family Begoniaceae
Plant: 10–14" tall.
Flower: 1 1/4" wide.
Description: Pink elongated cluster of bilaterally symmetrical flowers, 4 petals 1 1/4" x 1 1/4". Buds heart shaped. Stem red. Alternate waxy asymmetrical toothed leaves (1 1/4–2") wing-like, red veins, above each leaf where it joins stem are clusters of tiny red balls.
Habitat: Rock outcroppings, moist, sun. Elevation 5409'.
Range: Northern and central Mexico, Guatemala.
Comments: Photographed in August across the road from Paraiso del Oso near the Arroyo del Cerocahui.

• Familia Begoniaceae
Planta: de 25.4 a 35.5 cm de alto.
Flor: de 3.1 cm de ancho.
Descripción: Flores agrupadas en forma de racimo, bilateralmente simétricas, de color rosa, 4 pétalos de 3.1 cm x 3.1 cm. Yemas en forma de corazón. Tallo rojo. Hojas aceradas, asimétricas, dentadas, de 3.1 a 5 cm de largo, nervaduras rojas, provistas de pequeñas glándulas rojas en la base de la cada hoja.
Hábitat: Entre rocas, lugares húmedos, asoleados. Elevación 1649 m.
Distribución: Norte y centro de México, Guatemala.
Comentarios: Fotografiada en agosto cruzando el camino de Paraiso del Oso, cerca del Arroyo del Cerocahui.

alt Spring Checkerbloom/*Sidalcea*
eomexicana

Begonia, Agritos/*Begonia gracilis*

123

Pink Rounded Clusters

Crusea Diversifolia
Crusea wrightii

• Madder family Rubiaceae
Plant: 19" tall.
Flower: 1/8" wide.
Description: Pink rounded cluster of radially symmetrical flowers, 4 petals, surrounded by 4 or more bracts. Stem rough, dark red near bottom. Opposite, narrow lanceolate leaves 1–1 1/2" long, margins entire.
Habitat: Up from stream bed, rock and sand, moist, sun. Elevation 5471'.
Range: Chihuahua, Jalisco, Michoacán, Nayarit, Sonora in Mexico.
Comments: Photographed in September at Tascate between Paraiso del Oso and Cerocahui.

• Familia Rubiaceae
Planta: de 48 cm de alto.
Flor: de 3 mm de ancho.
Descripción: Planta con una flor pequeña, de color rosa, radialmente simétrica, 4 pétalos redondos, sostenidos por 4 o más brácteas. Tallo rugoso, con la base de color rojo oscuro. Hojas opuestas, angostas, lanceoladas, de 2.5 a 3.8 cm de largo, márgenes enteros.
Hábitat: Orillas de arroyo, rocosas y arenosos, húmedas, asoleados. Elevación 1668 m.
Distribución: Chihuahua, Jalisco, Michoacán, Nayarit, Sonora en México.
Comentarios: Fotografiada en septiembre en Táscate entre Paraiso del Oso y Cerocahui.

Butterfly Mist
Ageratum corymbosum

• Aster family Asteraceae
Plant: 23" tall.
Flower: 3/8" wide.
Description: Lavender rounded cluster of small feathery flowers, 1" flower stems with green calyx that attaches with long purple stem. Opposite, arrow-shaped, toothed leaves 1–1 1/2" long, dark red center vein, rough texture.
Habitat: Side hill up from stream, loam, dry, sun. Elevation 5516'.
Range: West Texas, Arizona, New Mexico, Mexico.
Comments: Photographed in September between the first and second cave on the trail to Cave of Crosses near Paraiso del Oso, Cerocahui.

• Familia del girasol Asteraceae
Planta: de 58 cm de alto.
Flor: de 9 mm de ancho.
Descripción: Cabezuela formada por pequeñas flores liguladas de color lavanda, sobre pedúnculo de 2.5 cm de largo, sostenida por filarios verdes. Hojas opuestas, en forma de flecha, dentadas, de 2.5 a 3.8 cm de largo, nervaduras de color rojo oscuro, rugosas.
Hábitat: Pendiente sobre orilla del arroyo, suelo franco, seco, asoleado. Elevación 1681 m.
Distribución: Oeste de Texas, Arizona, Nuevo México, México.
Comentarios: Fotografiada en septiembre entre la primera y segunda cueva, camino a la Cueva de las Cruces, cerca de Paraiso del Oso, Cerocahui.

Crusea Diversifolia/*Crusea wrightii*

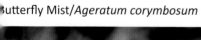
Butterfly Mist/*Ageratum corymbosum*

125

Pink Rounded Clusters

Cherry Sage
Salvia microphylla

• Mint family Lamiaceae
Plant: 26–30" tall.
Flower: 1/2" long, 3/8–1/2" wide.
Description: Magenta loose rounded cluster of bilaterally symmetrical 2 lipped tubular flowers, 1/4" long green calyx. Square woody stem. Lanceolate, opposite or only one side, toothed leaves 1/2–1" long. Smells like oregano.
Habitat: Side of road, rocky cliff, rock, damp, sun. Elevation 7021'.
Range: Arizona, California, and Chihuahua, Mexico.
Comments: Photographed in September on the road to Cerro Gallegos near La Cueva (basket cave).

• Familia de la menta Lamiaceae
Planta: de 66 a 76 cm de alto.
Flor: de 13 mm de largo, por 9 a 13 mm de ancho.
Descripción: Flores bilateralmente simétricas, en inflorescencia abierta, de color magenta, bilabiadas, tubulares, con un cáliz de 6 mm de largo. Tallo cuadrado. Hojas opuestas, lanceoladas, dentadas, de 1.3 a 2.5 cm de largo. Aroma a orégano.
Hábitat: Orillas de camino, acantilado rocoso, húmedas, asoleadas. Elevación 2140 m.
Distribución: Arizona, California y Chihuahua, México.
Comentarios: Fotografiada en septiembre sobre camino al Cerro Gallegos cerca de la Cueva.

Mountain Mock Vervain, Fringed Verbena
Glandularia elegans

• Verbena family Verbenaceae
Plant: 7–9" tall.
Flower: 5/8" wide.
Description: Fuchsia rounded cluster, radially symmetrical flowers, 5 united petals. Woody stem. Rough, opposite, deeply lobed leaves 1–2 1/2" long.
Habitat: Stream bed, rocky, damp/dry, sun. Elevation 5433'.
Range: Arizona, Texas, Mexico.
Comments: Photographed in September below Tortuga vista, near Paraiso del Oso, Cerocahui.

• Familia del Oreganillo Verbenaceae
Planta: de 17.5 a 22.5 cm de alto.
Flor: de 16 mm de ancho.
Descripción: Flores radialmente simétricas, de color rosa, agrupadas, 5 pétalos unidos. Tallo leñoso. Hojas opuestas, rugosas, partidas en lobulos, de 2.5 a 6.3 cm de largo.
Hábitat: Lecho de arroyo, rocoso, húmedo/seco, asoleado. Elevación 1656 m.
Distribución: Arizona, Texas, México.
Comentarios: Fotografiada en septiembre abajo de Tortuga vista, cerca de Paraiso del Oso, Cerocahui.

Cherry Sage/*Salvia microphylla*

Mountain Mock Vervain, Fringed Verbena/
Glandularia elegans

Pink Rounded Clusters

Leatherleaf Spiderwort
Tradescantia crassifolia

• Spiderwort family Commelinaceae
Plant: 12–18" tall.
Flower: 3/4" wide.
Description: Fuchsia loose rounded cluster of bilaterally symmetrical 3 petaled flowers, stamens protruding out of center. Many buds coming off 1/4" thick, dense, round stem growing between rocks. Alternate, clasping lanceolate leaves 3–4" long, fuzz underneath, margins entire.
Habitat: Rock cliff, dry, sun. Elevation 7021'.
Range: Texas, New Mexico, Mexico, Guatemala.
Comments: Photographed in September on the road to Cerro Gallegos near La Cueva (basket cave).

• Familia Commelinaceae
Planta: de 30 a 45 cm de alto.
Flor: de 19 mm de ancho.
Descripción: Flores de color rosa, bilateralmente simétricas, con 3 pétalos, y con estambres saliendo del centro. Muchas yemas saliendo de un tallo redondo, de 6 mm de grosor, creciendo entre las rocas. Hojas alternas, envainadas, lanceoladas, de 7.5 a 10 cm de largo, peludas en el envés, márgenes enteros.
Hábitat: Acantilado rocoso, seco, asoleado. Elevación 2140 m.
Distribución: Texas, Nuevo México, México, Guatemala.
Comentarios: Fotografiada en septiembre sobre camino al Cerro Gallegos cerca de la Cueva.

Leatherleaf Spiderwort/*Tradescantia crassifolia*

Part Six Purple Flowers

Purple Radially Symmetrical
Mountain Wood Sorrel
Oxalis alpina
- Wood sorrel family Oxalidaceae

Plant: 5" tall.
Flower: 1/2" long.
Description: Violet radially symmetrical tubular flower 1/2" long with flair, white throat. Leaves 1" wide, deeply notched leaflets, brownish chevrons.
Habitat: Moss on rock cliff on roadside, moist, sun. Elevation 6630'.
Range: Arizona, northern Mexico.
Comments: Photographed in August on the road coming out of the canyon from Urique.

- Familia Oxalidaceae

Planta: de 12.5 cm de alto.
Flor: de 13 mm de largo.
Descripción: Flor tubular de 1.3 cm de largo, color violeta, radialmente simétrica, con garganta blanca. Hojas palmeadamente compuestas, de 2.5 cm de largo, con foliolos profundamente hendidos, de color café.
Hábitat: Orillas de camino, sobre rocas con musgos, húmedas, asoleados. Elevación 2021 m.
Distribución: Arizona, norte de México.
Comentarios: Fotografiada en agosto en camino saliendo del cañón de Urique.

Solanum houstonii
- Nightshade family Solanaceae

Plant: 18" tall.
Flower: 3/4" wide.
Description: Violet, star-like, radially symmetrical flower, 5 united petals. Leaves alternate, bluish gray, ovate, 1 1/4–2 1/2", margins lobed. Stems have fine prickles.
Habitat: Roadside, dry, sun. Elevation 3006'.
Range: Southern U.S., northern Mexico.
Comments: Photographed in August on the roadside coming out of the canyon from Urique.

- Familia de la papa Solanaceae

Planta: de 45 cm de alto.
Flor: de 19 mm de ancho.
Descripción: Flor estrellada, violeta, radialmente simétrica, 5 petalos unidos. Hojas alternas, azul-grisaceas, ovadas, de 3.1 a 6.3 cm de largo, márgenes lobulados. Tallos espinosos.
Hábitat: Orillas de caminos, secas, asoleados. Elevación 916 m.
Distribución: Sur de USA, norte de México.
Comentarios: Fotografiada en agosto en camino saliendo del cañón de Urique.

Mountain Wood Sorrel/*Oxalis alpina*

Solanum houstonii

Purple Radially Symmetrical

Watermelon Nightshade
Solanum citrullifolium

- Nightshade family Solanaceae
Plant: 5 3/4" tall.
Flower: 1 3/4" wide.
Description: Violet radially symmetrical, star-like flower, 5 united petals, 5 anthers—4 yellow 1/4" long, 1 yellow green 1/2" long. Prominent yellow in center. Stems erect with prickles surrounding calyx. Leaves alternate, pinnate lobes, 1–1 1/4" long. Margins lobed. Back of leaves covered with hairs.
Habitat: On hillside edge of valley, soil loam and broken up volcanic rock, dry, sun. Elevation 7652'.
Range: Florida, Massachusetts, Oklahoma, Texas, Mexico.
Comments: Photographed in September after the right hand turn into San Ignacio valle, 2.5 miles from Creel.

- Familia de la papa Solanaceae
Planta: de 14.6 cm de alto.
Flor: de 4.4 cm de ancho.
Descripción: Flor estrellada, violeta, radialmente simétrica, 5 pétalos unidos, 5 anteras: 4 amarillos de 6 mm de largo y verde-amarillo de 1.3 cm de largo. Color amarillo prominente en el centro. Tallos erectos con espinas alrededor del cáliz. Hojas alternas, pinnadamente lobuladas, de 2.5 a 3.1 cm de largo, márgenes lobulados. El envés de las hojas velludo.
Hábitat: Orillas de pendiente del valle, suelo limoso, y roca volcánica quebrada, seco, asoleado. Elevación 2332 m.
Distribución: Florida, Massachusetts, Oklahoma, Texas, México.
Comentarios: Fotografiada en septiembre después de la vuelta a la derecha a San Ignacio, 4 km de Creel.

Morning Glory, Manto
Ipomoea hirsuta

- Morning glory family Convolvulaceae
Plant: Vine.
Flower: 1 1/2" long, 2 1/2" wide.
Description: Vine bearing large purple radially symmetrical funnel-shaped flowers, orchid centers, striations radiating out from center. Leaves alternate, 2" long, 3-lobed, margins smooth.
Habitat: Roadside, moist sand, sun. Elevation 5336'.
Range: Jalisco, Guadalajara, Chihuahua in Mexico.
Comments: Photographed in August on the roadside between Paraiso del Oso and Cerocahui.

- Familia de la jicama Convolvulaceae
Planta: Trepadora.
Flor: de 3.8 cm de largo, por 6.3 cm de ancho.
Descripción: Trepadora con grandes flores en forma de embudo, radialmente simétricas, de color morado, con rayas saliendo del centro. Hojas alternas, de 5 cm de largo, con 3 lobulos, márgenes enteros.
Hábitat: Orillas de camino, húmedas, arenosas, asoleadas. Elevación 1626 m.
Distribución: Jalisco, Guadalajara, Chihuahua en México.
Comentarios: Fotografiada en agosto sobre orillas de camino entre Paraiso del Oso y Cerocahui.

Watermelon Nightshade/*Solanum citrullifolium*

Morning Glory, Manto/*Ipomoea hirsuta*

Purple Radially Symmetrical
Morning Glory
Ipomoea pedicellaris

• Morning glory family Convolvulaceae
Plant: Vine.
Flower: 3 3/4" long, 4" wide.
Description: Deep violet radially symmetrical funnel-shaped flower, 5 connected sections that radiate into points, throat magenta/deep pink, back of flower light lavender. Vine that grows on large shrubs. Leaves opposite and alternate, heart shaped, 1–1 3/4" long. Margins entire.
Habitat: Along river bed, rock and sand, damp during rainy season, sun. Elevation 2080'.
Range: Honduras, Mexico.
Comments: Photographed in September in Arroyo Los Tachos, Batopilas.

• Familia de la jicama Convolvulaceae
Planta: Trepadora.
Flor: de 9.4 cm de largo, por 10 cm de ancho.
Descripción: Flores muy violetas, grandes, radialmente simétricas en forma de embudo, con 5 pétalos unidos, acuminados, garganta de color magenta a morado oscuro, de color lavanda en el exterior. Una trepadora que crece sobre arbustos grandes. Hojas opuestas y alternas, en forma de corazón, de 2.5 a 4.4 cm de largo, márgenes enteros.
Hábitat: A lo largo del río, rocoso y arenoso, húmedo, asoleado. Elevación 634 m.
Distribución: Honduras, México.
Comentarios: Fotografiada en septiembre en el Arroyo Los Tachos, Batopilas.

Purple Bilaterally Symmetrical
Pinewoods Spiderwort, Lágrima de la niña
Tradescantia pinetorum

• Spiderwort family Commelinaceae
Plant: 10–30" tall.
Flower: 3/4" wide.
Description: Light violet bilaterally symmetrical 3 petal flower, cluster at top of stem. Leaves alternate, 1–2 1/2" long, linear and very narrow, margins entire.
Habitat: Top of slope on volcanic rock, sand, moist, sun. Elevation 5521'.
Range: Arizona, New Mexico, Rocky Mountains, Mexico.
Comments: Photographed in August on the east side of the road between Paraiso del Oso and Bahuichivo.

• Familia Commelinaceae
Planta: de 25.4 a 76 cm de alto.
Flor: de 19 mm de ancho.
Descripción: Flor violeta pálida, bilateralmente simétrica, con 3 pétalos, agrupadas al extremo del tallo floral. Hojas alternas, de 2.5 a 6.3 cm de largo, lineares y muy angostas, márgenes enteros.
Hábitat: Arriba de una pendiente sobre roca volcanica, arenoso, húmedo, asoleado. Elevación 1683 m.
Distribución: Arizona, Nuevo México, Las Rocallosas, México.
Comentarios: Fotografiada en agosto en el lado este del camino entre Paraiso del Oso y Bahuichivo.

Morning Glory/*Ipomoea pedicellaris*

Pinewoods Spiderwort, Lágrima de la niña/*Tradescantia pinetorum*

Purple Bilaterally Symmetrical

Blue Mudplantain, Ducksalad
Heteranthera limosa

• Water hyacinth family Pontederiaceae
Plant: Aquatic.
Flower: 1" long, 1" wide.
Description: Vine bearing small purple and white bilaterally symmetrical flowers, 6 petals, yellow near center. Leaves alternate, ovate, 1 1/2" long, margins entire. Plant grows in mass in shallow water.
Habitat: Roadside ditch with water and sun. Elevation 5402'.
Range: U.S., West Indies, Central and South America, Mexico.
Comments: Photographed in August on the roadside between Paraiso del Oso and Cerocahui.

• Familia Pontederiaceae
Planta: Acuatica.
Flor: de 25 mm de largo, por 25 mm de ancho.
Descripción: Acuática Rastrera con pequeñas flores moradas y blancas, bilateralmente simétricas, 6 pétalos, amarillos cerca del centro. Hojas alternas, ovadas, de 3.8 cm de largo, márgenes enteros. Crece en masa en aguas someras.
Hábitat: Zanja a la orilla de camino con agua y asoleado. Elevación 1647 m.
Distribución: USA, Oceanía, Centro y Sur América, México.
Comentarios: Fotografiada en agosto sobre orilla de camino entre Paraiso del Oso y Cerocahui.

Widow's Tears
Achimenes mexicana

• Gesneria family Gesneriaceae
Plant: 9" tall.
Flower: 1–3" long, 2" wide.
Description: Deep cobalt violet bilaterally symmetrical flower, funnel-shaped, rimmed with 5 lobes, white throat. Leaves opposite, ovate, 3–4" long, margins toothed. Hairy leaves.
Habitat: Volcanic ryolitic tuff rock slope above stream under rock ledge, loam, damp, semi-shade. Elevation 5479'.
Range: Central America, Caribbean, Mexico.
Comments: Photographed in August across the road from Paraiso del Oso on rocks after crossing the bridge of the Arroyo del Tortuga, Cerocahui.

• Familia Gesneriaceae
Planta: de 22.5 cm de alto.
Flor: de 2.5 a 7.5 cm de largo, por 5 cm de ancho.
Descripción: Flor en forma de embudo, bilateralmente simétrica, de color violeta cobalto, pétalos unidos marcados por 5 lobulos, garganta blanca. Hojas opuestas, ovadas, de 7.5 a 10 cm de largo, márgenes dentados. Hojas peludas.
Hábitat: Pendiente con roca volcánica arriba del arroyo, suelo limoso, húmedo, semí-sombreado. Elevación 1670 m.
Distribución: América central, Caribe, México.
Comentarios: Fotografiada en agosto en el camino de Paraiso del Oso sobre rocas después de cruzar el puente del Arroyo del Tortuga, Cerocahui.

Blue Mudplantain, Ducksalad/*Heteranthera limosa*

Widow's Tears /*Achimenes mexicana*

Purple Elongated Clusters

Salvia muscarioides

- Mint family Lamiaceae
Plant: 15–21" tall.
Flower cluster: 1–3" long.
Description: Purple elongated cluster of bilaterally symmetrical flowers. Opposite linear leaves 1 3/4–2" long, closer together near bottom of stem, margins entire.
Habitat: Rim of canyon, rocky ground, shallow layer of soil, semi-moist, loam, sun. Elevation 7805'.
Range: Chihuahua, Mexico.
Comments: Photographed in September at Cerro Gallegos, upper lookout.

- Familia de la menta Lamiaceae
Planta: de 37.5 a 53 cm de alto.
Grupo de flores: de 2.5 a 7.5 cm de largo.
Descripción: Flores agrupadas sobre un tallo alargado, de color morado, bilateralmente simétricas. Hojas opuestas, lineares, de 4.4 a 5 cm de largo, más compactas hacia la base del tallo principal, márgenes enteros.
Hábitat: Orilla del cañón, suelo rocoso, someros, semí-húmedo, limoso, asoleado. Elevación 2379 m.
Distribución: Chihuahua, México.
Comentarios: Fotografiada en septiembre en el Cerro Gallegos, parte de arriba.

Blue Pygmyflower

Monnina wrightii

- Milkwort family Polygalaceae
Plant: 30–36" tall.
Flower cluster: 4–6" long.
Description: Narrow purple elongated cluster of bilaterally symmetrical flowers. Alternate, lanceolate leaves 3/4–2" long, margins entire.
Habitat: Mostly barren volcanic plateau, rocky base with some soil, semi-arid, sun. Elevation 5639'.
Range: Arizona, New Mexico, and Chihuahua, Mexico.
Comments: Photographed in September at El Ranchito up on the mountain behind Paraiso del Oso, Cerocahui.

- Familia Polygalaceae
Planta: de 76 a 91 cm de alto.
Grupo de flores: de 10 a 15 cm de largo.
Descripción: Flores agrupadas, terminales, de color morado, bilateralmente simétricas. Hojas alternas, lanceoladas, de 1.9 a 5 cm de largo, márgenes enteros.
Hábitat: Meseta con rocas volcánicas, suelo someros, semí-seco, asoleado. Elevación 1719 m.
Distribución: Arizona, Nuevo México y Chihuahua, México.
Comentarios: Fotografiada en septiembre en el Ranchito, en el cerro atras de Paraiso del Oso, Cerocachui.

Salvia muscarioides

Blue Pygmyflower/*Monnina wrightii*

139

Purple Elongated Clusters

Salvia goldmanii

• Mint family Lamiaceae
Plant: 48" tall.
Flower: 3/4" long, 1/4" wide.
Description: Violet elongated cluster in whorl, bilaterally symmetrical flowers, 2 lipped tubular shape—upper lip–hood, lower lip–2 lobed with white stripes leading into white throat. Calyx 1/4" long. Multi-stemmed, woody, hairs. Stiff leaves, opposite, lanceolate, larger leaves 1 1/4–2 1/4" long, smaller ones 1/2–5/8" long. Margins toothed.
Habitat: Sloped cliff leading to ravine, rocky, damp, shade/sun. Elevation 5480'.
Range: Chihuahua, Sinaloa, Sonora in Mexico.
Comments: Photographed in September on the trail to Huicochi (waterfall), half way from trailhead, Cerocahui.

• Familia de la menta Lamiaceae
Planta: de 122 cm de alto.
Flor: de 19 mm de largo, por 6 mm de ancho.
Descripción: Flores agrupadas, bilateralmente simétricas, tubulares, violetas sobre tallo alargado, bilabiadas, labio superior en forma de capuchón, labio inferior con 2 lobulos, con rayas blancas hacia la garganta. Cáliz de 6 mm de largo. Tallos numerosos, leñosos, velludos. Hojas rígidas, opuestas, lanceoladas, variando en tamaño desde de 1.3 cm hasta 6.3 cm, márgenes dentados.
Hábitat: Pendiente arriba de richuelo, rocosa, húmeda, sombreada/asoleado. Elevación 1670 m.
Distribución: Chihuahua, Sinaloa, Sonora en México.
Comentarios: Fotografiada en septiembre sobre camino a la Cascada de Huicochi, Cerocahui.

Salvia longispicata

• Mint family Lamiaceae
Plant: 28–36" tall.
Flower: 3/8" long, 3/8" wide.
Description: Lavender elongated cluster, bilaterally symmetrical 2 lipped tubular flowers—upper lip like a hairy hood, lower 2 lobed, white throat between upper and lower. Multi-stemmed, small shrub-like. Leaves opposite, lanceolate, 3/4–2 1/2" long. Margins toothed.
Habitat: River bed, rock and sand, wet, sun/shade. Elevation 1961'.
Range: Chiapas and Chihuahua in Mexico.
Comments: Photographed in September in Arroyo Los Tachos, Batopilas.

• Familia de la menta Lamiaceae
Planta: de 71 a 91 cm de alto.
Flor: de 9 mm de largo, por 9 mm de ancho.
Descripción: Flores bilateralmente simétricas, tubulares, bilabiadas, lavandas, agrupadas, labio superior formando un capuchón peludo, labio inferior con 2 lobulos, garganta blanca entre los dos labios. Tallos numerosos, algo leñosos. Hojas opuestas, lanceoladas, de 1.9 a 6.3 cm de largo, márgenes dentados.
Hábitat: Lecho de río, rocoso y arenoso, húmedo, asoleado/sombreado. Elevación 598 m.
Distribución: Chiapas y Chihuahua en México.
Comentarios: Fotografiada en septiembre en el Arroyo Los Tachos, Batopilas.

Salvia goldmanii

Salvia longispicata

Purple Elongated Clusters

Lupine
Lupinus confusus

• Pea family Fabaceae
Plant: 10–14" tall.
Flower: 3/8" long, 1/2" wide.
Description: Purple, magenta, and white elongated cluster, bilaterally symmetrical flowers, long dense racemes. Leaves alternate, palmately compound with leaflets arranged like wheel spokes 1/2–1 1/4" long, margins entire.
Habitat: Roadside, sand and clay, moist, sun. Elevation 8040'.
Range: Oregon and Chihuahua, Mexico.
Comments: Photographed in September on the road to Sinforosa Canyon, 9.3 miles from Guachochi.

• Familia del frijol Fabaceae
Planta: de 25.6 a 35.5 cm de alto.
Flor: de 9 mm de largo, por 13 mm de ancho.
Descripción: Flores bilateralmente simétricas de color morado, magenta y blanco, sobre racimos densos y alargados. Hojas alternas, palmeadamente compuestas, con los foliolos arreglados como rayos de una rueda, de 1.3 a 3.1 cm de largo, márgenes enteros.
Hábitat: Orillas de camino, arenosos y arcillosas, húmedas, asoleados. Elevación 2451 m.
Distribución: Oregon y Chihuahua, México.
Comentarios: Fotografiada en septiembre, camino al cañón de la Sinforosa, 15 km de Guachochi.

Lupine
Lupinus montanus

• Pea family Fabaceae
Plant: 24–32" tall.
Flower: 1/2–5/8" long, 3/4" wide.
Description: White, violet, and darker violet elongated cluster of bilaterally symmetrical flowers, long dense racemes. Leaves palmately compound with leaflets arranged like wheel spokes 1–1 1/4" long, margins entire.
Habitat: Side of road, rock and sand, somewhat damp, sun. Elevation 6891'.
Range: Guatemala, Peru, northern and central Mexico.
Comments: Photographed in September on the road from Cerocahui to San Isidro, at km 20.

• Familia del frijol Fabaceae
Planta: de 60 a 81 cm de alto.
Flor: de 13 a 16 mm de largo, por 19 mm de ancho.
Descripción: Flores sobre racimos densos y alargados, de color blanco, violeta a azul, bilateralmente simétricas. Hojas alternas, palmeadamente compuestas con foliolos arreglados en rayos de una rueda, de 2.5 a 3.1 cm de largo, márgenes enteros.
Hábitat: Orilla de camino, rocosa y arenoso, algo húmeda, asoleado. Elevación 2100 m.
Distribución: Guatemala, Perú, norte y centro de México.
Comentarios: Fotografiada en septiembre, camino de Cerocahui a San Isidro en el km 20.

Lupine/*Lupinus confusus*

Lupine/*Lupinus montanus*

Purple Elongated Clusters

Bellflower Beardtongue, Jarita
Penstemon campanulatus

• Figwort family Scrophulariaceae
Plant: 10–17 1/2" tall.
Flower: 1/2–3/4" wide.
Description: Deep cobalt violet loose elongated cluster of bilaterally symmetrical flowers in whorls, white throat. Also seen in manganese violet. Flared tubular flower with 5 lobes—2 on top that bend up, 3 on bottom spreading downward—1/2–3/4" wide, 1/2–3/4" high, 1" long. Leaves opposite, 2" long, pointed lanceolate then smaller leaves opposite main leaves, margins entire.
Habitat: Between rocks, sand and red clay, moist or dry, sun. Elevation 5673' to 7716'.
Range: Sonora, Chihuahua, Durango in Mexico, and Guatemala.
Comments: Photographed in August off the east side of the road between Paraiso del Oso and Bahuichivo.

• Familia Scrophulariaceae
Planta: de 25.4 a 44.3 cm de alto.
Flor: de 13 a 19 mm de ancho.
Descripción: Flores arregladas en verticilos, bilateralmente simétricas, de color violeta cobalto, tubulares, con garganta blanca, terminando con 5 pétalos, en dos labios: 2 superiores doblados hacia arriba y 3 inferiores hacia abajo, de 13 a 19 mm de ancho y 2.5 cm de largo. Hojas opuestas, lanceoladas, acuminadas, hojas más pequeñas opuestas a las hojas principales, márgenes enteros.
Hábitat: Entre rocas, suelo arenoso y arcilla roja, húmedo o seca, asoleado. Elevación 1729 a 2352 m.
Distribución: Sonora, Chihuahua, Durango en México, y Guatemala.
Comentarios: Fotografiada en agosto sobre orilla este del camino entre Paraiso del Oso y Bahuichivo.

Jarritos
Penstemon campanulatus subsp. Chihuahuensis

• Figwort family Scrophulariaceae
Plant: 12" tall.
Flower: 1" long, 3/4" wide.
Description: Violet, loose elongated cluster, bilaterally symmetrical flowers, short, squat tube with 2 upper lobes, 3 lower lobes, white throat, deep purple stripes to guide insect into flower, prominent pistil and stamens. Leaves opposite, linear, 1–1 1/2" long. Margins slightly toothed.
Habitat: Roadside, next to field, sandy loam, moist, sun. Elevation 7696'.
Range: Chihuahua, Durango, Sonora in Mexico.
Comments: Photographed in September at Wetosakachi, 3.1 miles from Creel.

• Familia Scrophulariaceae
Planta: de 30 cm de alto.
Flor: de 25 mm de largo, por 19 mm de ancho.
Descripción: Flores bilateralmente simétricas, violetas, pétalos unidos formando un tubo corto, bilabiadas: 2 labios superiores y 3 inferiores, garganta blanca, rayas de color morado oscuro guiando a los insectos hacia adentro de la flor; pistilo y estambres salientes. Hojas opuestas, lineares, de 2.5 a 3.8 cm de largo, márgenes ligeramente dentados.
Hábitat: Orillas de camino, cerca de un campo, arenosos, limosas, húmedas y asoleados. Elevación 2346 m.
Distribución: Chihuahua, Durango, Sonora en México.
Comentarios: Fotografiada en septiembre en Wetosakachi, 5 km de Creel.

Bellflower Beardtongue, Jarita/*Penstemon campanulatus*

Jarritos/*Penstemon campanulatus subsp. Chihuahuensis*

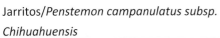

Purple Elongated Clusters

Apache Lobelia, Bluebell Lobelia
Lobelia anatina

• Bellflower family Campanulaceae
Plant: 6–20" tall.
Flower: 1" long, 3/4" wide.
Description: Violet elongated cluster, bilaterally symmetrical flower, 1/4" tube then 3 lower flared petals, 2 upper narrow petals curved back. Leaves alternate, linear 1/2–3 1/2" long. Margins toothed.
Habitat: Fertile plain, farmland, growing along fence line, topsoil, moist, sun. Elevation 8160'.
Range: Arizona, New Mexico, and Chihuahua, Mexico.
Comments: Photographed in September on the road to Sinforosa Canyon, 6.8 miles from Guachochi.

• Familia Campanulaceae
Planta: de 15 a 50 cm de alto.
Flor: de 25 mm de largo, por 19 mm de ancho.
Descripción: Flores bilateralmente simétricas, violetas, pétalos unidos formando un tubo de 6 mm de largo, bilabiado: 3 labios inferiores y 2 superiores doblados hacia arriba. Hojas alternas, lineares, de 1.3 a 8.8 cm de largo, márgenes dentados.
Hábitat: Llano fértil, tierra de cultivo, a lo largo de un cerco, suelo húmedo, asoleado. Elevación 2487 m.
Distribución: Arizona, Nuevo México y Chihuahua, México.
Comentarios: Fotografiada en septiembre sobre camino al cañón de la Sinforosa, 11 km de Guachochi.

Spiked Larkspur, Umatilla Larkspur
Delphinium scopulorum

• Buttercup family Ranunculaceae
Plant: 3–5' tall.
Flower: 1" long, 3/4" wide.
Description: Purple elongated cluster, bilaterally symmetrical flower, 5 sepals, petal-like, backward projecting spur, 2 petals and hood with hairs surrounding stamens. Leaves alternate, pinnately divided into narrow forked lobes 3/4–1 1/2" long.
Habitat: Fertile plain, farmland, growing along fence line, topsoil, moist, sun. Elevation 8160'.
Range: California, Idaho, Nevada, Oregon, Washington, and Chihuahua, Mexico.
Comments: Photographed in September on the road to Sinforosa Canyon, 6.8 miles from Guachochi.

• Familia Ranunculaceae
Planta: de 90 a 150 cm de alto.
Flor: de 25 mm de largo, por 19 mm de ancho.
Descripción: Flores bilateralmente simétricas, moradas, 5 pétalos cada uno con una espuela, 2 pétalos y el capuchón con vellosidades alrededor de los estambres. Hojas pinnadamente divididas en lobulos angostos, de 1.9 a 3.8 cm de largo.
Hábitat: Llano fértil, tierra de cultivo, a lo largo de un cerco, suelo húmedo, asoleado. Elevación 2487 m.
Distribución: California, Idaho, Nevada, Oregon, Washington, y Chihuahua, México.
Comentarios: Fotografiada en septiembre sobre camino al cañón de la Sinforosa, 11 km de Guachochi.

Apache Lobelia, Bluebell Lobelia/
Lobelia anatina

piked Larkspur, Umatilla Larkspur/
Delphinium scopulorum

147

Purple Elongated Clusters

Sonoran Beardtongue
Penstemon stenophyllus

• Figwort family Scrophulariaceae
Plant: 16–20" tall.
Flower: 1 1/2" long, 3/4–1" wide.
Description: Magenta to purple elongated cluster, 5 lobed funnel shaped bilaterally symmetrical flowers. Thin stem. Opposite, very thin linear leaves 1–4 1/2" long, margins entire.
Habitat: Wooded area long trail, rocky, damp, semi-shade. Elevation 5710'.
Range: Arizona, New Mexico, and Chihuahua, Durango, San Luis Potosí, Sonora, Zacatecas in Mexico.
Comments: Photographed in September near the high vista on the Tortuga trail, Cerocahui.

• Familia Scrophulariaceae
Planta: de 41 a 50 cm de alto.
Flor: de 38 mm de largo, por 19 a 25 mm de ancho.
Descripción: Flores bilateralmente simétricas, magentas, 5 pétalos unidos formando un embudo. Tallo delgado. Hojas opuestas, muy delgados, lineares, de 2.5 a 11.5 cm de largo, márgenes enteros.
Hábitat: Área boscosa a lo largo del camino, rocosa, humeda, semí-sombreada. Elevación 1740 m.
Distribución: Arizona, Nuevo México, y Chihuahua, Durango, San Luis Potosí, Sonora, Zacatecas en México.
Comentarios: Fotografiada en septiembre cerca de Alta vista sobre camino a Tortuga, Cerocahui.

Purple Rounded Clusters

Not Yet Identified

• Mint family Lamiaceae
Plant: 8–12" high.
Flower: 3/8" long, 1/4" wide.
Description: Light violet rounded cluster with whorls of flower heads, bilaterally symmetrical 2 lipped tubular flower-upper hood, lower 4 lobed. White stripes leading into white throat. Flower clusters surrounded by sheath. Leaves opposite, heart shaped, 2 longer 3/4–1", 4 shorter 1/4". Margins toothed.
Habitat: Along side trail, rock, compost, damp, shade/sun. Elevation 5490'.
Range: Chihuahua, Mexico.
Comments: Photographed in September on the trail to Huicochi (waterfall), two-thirds of the way from trailhead, Cerocahui.

• Familia de menta Lamiaceae
Planta: de 20 a 30 cm de alto.
Flor: de 9 mm de largo, por 6 mm de ancho.
Descripción: Flores agrupadas en verticilos, de color violeta pálido, bilateralmente simétricas, tubulares, bilabiadas: un labio superior en forma de capuchón, y 4 inferiores. Rayas blancas en la garganta blanca. Flores sostenidas por espatas. Hojas opuestas, en forma de corazón: 2 grande de 19 a 25 mm de largo y mas pequeñas de 6 mm de largo, márgenes dentados.
Hábitat: A lo largo del camino, rocoso, con mantilla, húmedo, sombreado/asoleado. Elevación 1673 m.
Distribución: Chihuahua, México.
Comentarios: Fotografiada en septiembre sobre camino a la Cascada de Huicochi, Cerocahui.

Sonoran Beardtongue/*Penstemon stenophyllus*

Not Yet Identified

Purple Rounded Clusters

Common Selfheal
Prunella vulgaris

• Mint family Lamiaceae
Plant: 4" tall.
Flower: 1" long, 1" wide.
Description: Deep violet rounded cluster made up of radially symmetrical 2-lipped tubular flowers, 1/2" long, surrounding dark red flower head, prominent white hairs, all held by green cup-shaped calyx. Leaves opposite, ovate, 1 1/4" long. Margins entire.
Habitat: Hillside on edge of valley, soil loam with broken up volcanic rock, dry, sun. Elevation 7652'.
Range: All of U.S. including Alaska and Hawaii, Mexico.
Comments: Photographed in September after the right hand turn into San Ignacio valle, 2.5 miles from Creel.

• Familia de la menta Lamiaceae
Planta: de 10 cm de alto.
Flor: de 25 mm de largo, por 25 mm de ancho.
Descripción: Flores bilateralmente simétricas, agrupadas, tubulares, bilabiadas, de 13 mm de largo, cáliz verde con vellosidades blancas. Hojas opuestas, ovadas, de 3.1 cm de largo. Márgenes enteros.
Hábitat: Loma sobre orilla de un valle, suelo limoso con rocas volcánicas quebradas, seco, asoleado. Elevación 2332 m.
Distribución: Todo USA incluyendo Alaska y Hawaii, México.
Comentarios: Fotografiada en septiembre despues de la vuelta a la derecha hacia el valle de San Ignacio, 4 km de Creel.

Common Selfheal/*Prunella vulgaris*

Part Seven Blue Flowers

Blue Radially Symmetrical

Eye of the Viper, Ojo de Vibora
Evolvulus alsinoides

• Morning glory family Convolvulaceae
Plant: 10–16" tall.
Flower: 1/2" wide.
Description: Blue radially symmetrical flower, 5 united petals, white eye. Grayish hairs, slender erect stems or spreading on ground. Leaves alternate, linear, 1/2–1" long. Margins entire.
Habitat: River bed, very sandy and rocky, wet, sun. Elevation 1925'.
Range: Arizona east to Texas and south into Mexico.
Comments: Photographed in September in Arroyo Los Tachos, Batopilas.

• Familia de la jicama Convolvulaceae
Planta: de 25.4 a 41 cm de alto.
Flor: de 13 mm de ancho.
Descripción: Flores radialmente simétricas, de color azul, 5 petalos, ojo blanco. Tallos rastreros a erectos, canosos. Hojas alternas, lineares, de 13 a 25 mm de largo. Márgenes enteros.
Hábitat: Lecho de río, muy arenoso y pedregoso, húmedo, asoleado. Elevación 587 m.
Distribución: Este de Arizona a Texas y sur hasta México.
Comentarios: Fotografiada en septiembre en el Arroyo Los Tachos, Batopilas.

Blue Bilaterally Symmetrical

Slender Dayflower, Hierba de Pollo
Commelina erecta

• Spiderwort family Commelinaceae
Plant: 4–8" high.
Flower: 3/8" long, 5/8" wide.
Description: Blue bilaterally symmetrical flower, 3 petals—2 upper ear-like blue petals, 1 smaller lower lobed translucent petal that emerges from boat-shaped bract. Leaves lanceolate, clasping, 1 1/2–3" long. Margins entire.
Habitat: Creek bed, rock and sand, wet, sun. Elevation 1910'.
Range: Colorado, Arizona, New Mexico, Texas, eastern United States, and Chihuahua, Mexico.
Comments: Photographed in September in Arroyo Los Tachos, Batopilas.

• Familia Commelinaceae
Planta: de 10 a 20 cm de alto.
Flor: de 9 mm de largo, por 16 mm de ancho.
Descripción: Flores azules, bilateralmente simétricas, 3 pétalos, 2 superiores azules y 1 inferior blanco, saliendo de una espata. Hojas lanceoladas, envainadas, de 3.8 a 7.5 cm de largo, márgenes enteros.
Hábitat: Lecho de arroyo, rocoso y arenoso, húmedo, asoleado. Elevación 582 m.
Distribución: Colorado, Arizona, Nuevo México, Texas, este de USA, y Chihuahua, México.
Comentarios: Fotografiada en septiembre en el Arroyo Los Tachos, Batopilas.

Eye of the Viper, Ojo de Vibora/
Evolvulus alsinoides

Slender Dayflower, Hierba de Pollo/
Commelina erecta

Blue Bilaterally Symmetrical

Day Flower, Yerba del Pollo
Commelina tuberosa

• Spiderwort family Commelinaceae
Plant: 12–18" tall.
Flower: 3/4" long, 1" wide.
Description: Various shades of blue bilaterally symmetrical flower, 3 petals, flowers emerge from asymmetrical boat-shaped bract that encloses groups of flower buds. Clasping lanceolate leaves, 2 1/4–4" long, margins entire.
Habitat: Rock outcroppings, sandy or loam soil, moist or dry, sun. Elevation 5400'.
Range: Peru, Guatemala, Nicaragua, Honduras, Bolivia, Mexico.
Comments: Photographed in August along the Arroyo del Ranchito behind Paraiso del Oso, Cerocahui.

• Familia Commelinaceae
Planta: de 30 a 45 cm de alto.
Flor: de 19 mm de largo, por 25 mm de ancho.
Descripción: Flores bilateralmente simétricas, azules, 3 petalos, saliendo de una espata. Hojas envainadas, lanceoladas, de 5.7 a 10 cm de largo, márgenes enteros.
Hábitat: Rocas, suelo arenoso o limoso, húmedo o seco, asoleado. Elevación 1646 m.
Distribución: Perú, Guatemala, Nicaragua, Honduras, Bolivia, México.
Comentarios: Fotografiada en agosto a lo largo del Arroyo del Ranchito atras de Paraiso del Oso, Cerocahui.

Day Flower, Yerba del Pollo/*Commelina tuberosa*

Bibliography

Chapman, William K., Valeria A. Chapman, Alan E. Bessette, Arleen Rainis Bessette, and Douglas R. Pens. *Wildflowers of New York in Color*. Syracuse, New York: Syracuse University Press, 1998.

Copper Canyons History...the land, the people, and the train. El Paso, Texas: Native Trails L.L.C. http://nativetrails.com/information/history.htm

Greene, Kim, and Don Greene. *Visit the Tarahumara Indians of The Copper Canyon, Chihuahua, Mexico*. Adventure Learning Foundation, 2003. http://questconnect.org/tara_home.htm

Loughmiller, Campbell, and Lynn Loughmiller. *Texas Wildflowers: A Field Guide*. Austin: University of Texas Press, 1984.

Noble, John, Susan Forsyth, Ben Greensfelder, Morgan Konn, Monica Lepe, James Lyon, Michele Matter, Alan Murphy, Andrew Dean Nystrom, Vivek Waglé, and Allison Wright. *Mexico: Lonely Planet*. Victoria, Australia: Lonely Planet Publications Pty Ltd, 2002.

Schmidt, Robert H. *Maps and Guide to the Chihuahua-Pacific Railroad*. El Paso, Texas: International Map Company.

Schmidt, Robert H. *Sierra Tarahumara: Barrancas del Cobre*. El Paso, Texas: International Map Company, 1996.

The Sierra Madre Occidental: Major Biotic Communities. The International BioPark Foundation. http://biopark.org/sierramadre.html

Spellenberg, R. *The Audubon Society Field Guide to North American Wildflowers, Western Region*. New York: Alfred A. Knopf, 2001.

INDEX

Italic page number denotes illustration